The Rational Kernel of the Hegelian Dialectic

TRANSMISSION

Transmission denotes the transfer of information, objects or forces from one place to another, from one person to another. Transmission implies urgency, even emergency: a line humming, an alarm sounding, a messenger bearing news. Through Transmission interventions are supported, and opinions overturned. Transmission republishes classic works in philosophy, as it publishes works that re-examine classical philosophical thought. Transmission is the name for what takes place.

The Rational Kernel of the Hegelian Dialectic

Translations, introductions and commentary on a text by Zhang Shiying

Alain Badiou
Joël Bellassen
Louis Mossot

Edited and translated by
Tzuchien Tho

re.press

PO Box 40, Prahran, 3181, Melbourne, Australia
http://www.re-press.org

National Library of Australia Cataloguing-in-Publication Data

Badiou, Alain.

The rational kernel of the Hegelian dialectic /
Alain Badiou; Tzuchien Tho, editor and translator.

9780980819762 (pbk.)
9780980819779 (ebook : pdf)

Series: Transmission.

Includes bibliographical references.

Philosophy, Marxist. Ideology. Dialectical materialism.

Other Authors/Contributors:
Joël Bellassen, Louis Mossot, Tho, Tzuchien.

320.5315

Designed and Typeset by *A&R*

Printed on-demand in Australia, the United Kingdom and the United States
This book is produced sustainably using plantation timber, and printed in the destination market on demand reducing wastage and excess transport.

Contents

Acknowledgements

This project could not have been completed without the tremendous help, encouragement, kindness and love shown to me not only by my partner Amy Anderson-Tho and my family but also by friends, comrades and colleagues: Benjamin Bishop, Patricia Goldsworthy, Krisha McCune, Priyanka Pandit, Evans Chan, Oliver Feltham, Giuseppe Bianco, Pietro Bianchi, Samo Tomšič, Avigail Moss, Eli Noé, Z. Luke Fraser, Dhruv Jain, Colin McQuillan, Frank Ruda, Jan and Marie Bergstrom. I would also like to thank the now fatally endangered Jan Van Eyck Academie in Maastricht Netherlands for supporting my research during this period. Its director, Koen Brams, the advisors in the theory department, Katja Diefenbach, Dominiek Hoens and Mladen Dolar as well as the technical and administrative staff not only provided the infrastructure but also afforded us the positive freedom necessary to create and re-create such a rare space of intellectual intensity, rigor and productivity. I would also like to thank Paul Ashton and Justin Clemens at re.press not only for their friendship but also for the patience and energy that they have taken to the project. Of course none of this would have been possible without Alain Badiou's decades of work and his generous friendship.

Introduction

One Divides into Two? Dividing the Conditions

Tzuchien Tho

Much like the *Concept of Model*, interest in this English translation and reediting of Alain Badiou's *Rational Kernel of the Hegelian Dialectic*[1] is no doubt due to its status as an *early* text of the French philosopher. This text, as with his other works from the same period, represents one among many phases in his intellectual development which may serve as a valuable quasi-archival resource by which to interpret the roots of his more recent systematic philosophy. In particular, Badiou frequently refers to the events of May '68 as his 'road to Damascus' in his political and intellectual trajectory, wrenching him from a theoreticist *Normalien* disposition to a decade of political militancy and estrangement from the philosophical mainstream.[2] Judging from his intellectual work during the 'red years' [*les années rouges*], roughly from 1968 to 1979, a period which includes the present volume, Badiou radically broke with his earlier interests in formal logic and mathematics and concentrated his efforts on political thought. Hegel, Marx, Lenin and Mao replaced his earlier references to Cantor, Frege, Von Neuman and Robinson.[3] Regardless of the many details that

1. *The Rational Kernel of the Hegelian Dialectic* will hereafter be referred to as Rational Kernel.

2. Alain Badiou, *Théorie de la contradiction*, Paris, Maspero, 1975, p. 9.

3. While I do point to something of a radical shift in Badiou's intellectual path, there is no doubt that mathematics never departed from Badiou's work. Yet, one might compare the rather negative assessment of mathematics in *Rational Kernel* with the energetic albeit limited use of set theory and topology in *Theory of the Subject* which overlaps with the former text. See Alain

may constitute the biographical retelling of Badiou's trajectory, subject to evaluation from all sides, what I hope to undertake in the following is to encircle a philosophical space within this transformation.[4] While *Concept of Model* marks a beginning, *Rational Kernel* traces a transformation that will be crucial for the work undertaken in *Theory of Subject* and outline the defining problematics of his mature work represented by the two volumes of *Being and Event*.

The original publication date of this text is 1978 and covers the very years represented in the dated seminar structure of the *Theory of the Subject*. Indeed, the very first sections of the book treat the two movements of the dialectic, its materialist kernel and its idealist shell. 'It is the kernel itself that is cracked, as in those peaches that are furthermore so irritating to eat whose hard internal object quickly cracks between one's teeth into two pivoting halves'.[5] It is in chewing the difficult fruit and cracking its bitter kernel that Badiou produced this first systematic work. Indeed, *Rational Kernel* and his other works in the 1970s can be read as lengthy footnotes to *Theory of the Subject*. Along with *Théorie de la Contradiction* and *De l'idéologie*, *Rational Kernel* (all published by François Maspero with his collaborator Sylvain Lazarus) serves as a third in a trilogy, a series of investigations that would crystallize in Badiou's first systematic work.

Theory of the Subject represents however a significant departure from his earlier 'Red trilogy'. Other than explicitly pointing to the insufficient reading of force in *Théorie de la Contradiction*, something that can also be said for the other works in the trilogy, Badiou presents, in *Theory of the Subject*, a degree of systematic articulation that only existed as disparate elements in his earlier writings.[6] From the systematic perspective of the *Theory of the Subject*, Badiou weaves together an edifice that will continue to be recast and reworked throughout his later work: political militancy and the state, subjective processes, the nature of placement and the out of place, algebra and topology, Mallarmé's chance, the twin notions of courage and justice, etc. Once in place, this systematic globality will continue to define Badiou's major works. Important lines of influence, transformation, reinvention and reinterpretation can easily be read between *Theory of the Subject*, *Being and Event*, *Logic of Worlds* and many other intermittent works. While *Theory of the Subject* might be seen as

---

Badiou, *Theory of the Subject*, trans. Bruno Bosteels, London, Continuum, 2009, p. 216-223.

4. See Alain Badiou, 'Philosophy as Biography', in *The Symptom*, 9, Fall 2008.

5. *Theory of the Subject*, p. 3.

6. *Theory of the Subject*, p. 141.

relatively disjointed and undeveloped from the perspective of the tightly argued meditations of *Being and Event*, it projected a vision of systematic philosophy that was not yet present in any of his earlier works.

Indeed, the systematic nature of Badiou's writings since *Theory of the Subject* characterizes the philosopher's enormous contribution to contemporary philosophy. The roots of this turn can no doubt be traced to a number of his concerns all the way back to *Concept of Model*. While philosophy since Kant's three critiques already prescribes a synonymous relation between philosophy and system, the enormous influence that Hegel and the Left-wing appropriation of Hegel exercised on Badiou, through Marx, Lenin and Mao, seems to oblige nothing short of systematicity for any philosophy worthy of the name. As Badiou himself later remarks in *Manifesto for Philosophy*, '[I]t is of the essence of philosophy to be systematic, and no philosopher has ever doubted this, from Plato to Hegel'.[7] At the same time as the text of *Rational Kernel* uncomfortably straddles the systematic drive of a philosophy grounded in dialectics and an interventionary division within the two sides of this dialectics itself (an idealist and a materialist side), it is through this straddling that Badiou opens the lacunae that will provide the shape of his future systematic project.

Important commentators in the Anglophone and Francophone commentary on Badiou have placed the important difference between the early and recent Badiou as one demarcated by the centrality of dialectics in his former work and the waning of this theme in his more recent contributions. This demarcation is not quite accurate. Among the central participants in this debate in Badiou scholarship, Bruno Bosteels has convincingly argued that the evolution of the dialectic in Badiou's work provides one in a number of continuities that stretch between his earliest works to his latest contributions. In Bosteels' 'Post-Maoism: Badiou and Politics', a masterfully written and thoroughly researched article chronicling Badiou's 'red years' and its consequences for today, he powerfully underlines the importance that the hallmarks of Badiou's 'red years' plays in his most recent works: the 'one divides into two' interpretation of the dialectic, the 'bottom-up' characterization of knowledge and the post-Leninist problematics of politics.[8] To use Badiou's more recent category

7. Alain Badiou, *Manifesto for Philosophy*, trans. Norman Madarasz, Albany, State University of New York Press, 1999, p. 65.

8. Bruno Bosteel's article 'Post-Maoism: Badiou and Politics' is one in a series of excellent essays and other documents (including original translation of fragments from Badiou's 'Red Years') whose publication in the journal *Positions: East Asia Cultures Critique* prepared for an international conference on Maoism and its legacy at the University of Washington in February 2006.

theoretical language, the interpretation promoted by Bosteels is one where it is the morphism of the dialectic that gives Badiou's early and recent work a continuous 'transcendental measure'.

Reading Badiou's 'red trilogy' through Bosteels' dialectic-centred interpretation however also gives one reason to pause and reconsider the demarcation between early and late in Badiou's trajectory. Bosteels rightly underlines the importance that Mao's emphasis on inquiry had not only on the revolutionary discourse in China since the 1930s but also the framework of Maoist activists and militants in Badiou's own European milieu. This emphasis on ground-up inquiry not only defined Mao's Yenan period but was also the driving force behind the Great Proletarian Cultural Revolution[9] and the Maoist activities in Europe from Godard's Dziga-Vertov projects to the 'Workerism' [*ouvriérisme*] of student participation in industrial work and organization. Local investigation, inquiry or enquiry (the English rendering of *enquête* by Feltham)[10] correspond to the basis of political work. No unifying principle, abstract ideal or revolutionary aesthetic can take its place. In turn, the necessary attention to the concrete, punctual and conjunctural reality defines radical political work of all stripes. Mao's particular emphasis on local investigation is indeed common place and does not provide a means to distinguish either the Chinese Red Guards of the GPCR, French Maoism, Italian Workerism [*operaismo*] or the particularity of Badiou's own political thought and activity. Along with this bottom-up common sense of political praxis, the reinvention of the dialectic and post-Leninism was widespread in different arenas from the Frankfurt School to Eurocommunism and the many minutely differential radical political programs in France, Germany and the rest of Europe. There is no doubt that Badiou was tremendously formed by his engagement with French Maoism and his careful study of Marxism-Leninism through the Maoist lens. This series of political dispositions however does not distinguish him from the enormous rethinking of politics (and philosophy) under a Maoist lens undertaken by militants and activists across the world, with widely differing results, that took place during the same period.

Among others at the conference were Mobo Gao, Wang Hui, Alessandro Russo and Yiching Wu who represent different aspects of a new wave of research on Maoism and its legacy for contemporary politics and philosophy. See Bruno Bosteels, 'Post-Maoism: Badiou and Politics', *Positions: East Asia Cultures Critique*, vol. 13, no. 3, 2005, pp. 575-634.

9. The Great Proletarian Cultural Revolution is hereafter referred to as GPCR.

10. Alain Badiou, *Being and Event*, trans. Oliver Feltham, London, Continuum, 2005, p. 329.

The legacy of Maoism is an equivocal one. The struggles in Latin America and that of South Asia do not resemble that of the Black Panthers or Chinese student-labor organizations. Its political-philosophical reach is also diverse, manifesting itself, within Badiou's immediate context, in post-Sartrean, post-Althusserian and anarchist forms. After the defeat of the Sixties, *L'Organization Politique*, the now defunct 'post-party' political organization which Badiou helped construct may also be said to partake in similar principles of Maoist intervention. No doubt, with the waning of the overarching organization, this organization remains active in its weekly meetings with *san-papiers* and faithful militants. While continued organization and struggle may not require a continuous name, it remains dubious whether the painstaking organization conducted by Badiou and his comrades in the *L'Organization Politique* may produce any palpable consequences, either in itself or through alliance with established forces or other *sans-papiers* organizations. The underdetermined context of the post-60s Thermidorian leaves much to be desired. This lack of political positivity is however not symmetrical in any sense to the enormous and systematic work that Badiou has produced in the wake of the lack of any 'new' in the political situation.

What I wish to underline is that, while the influence of Maoism and the focus of the GPCR on the dialectic are undeniable in Badiou's work, it neither provides a lens that allow us to distinguish him from other thinkers in the similar conjuncture nor a means to analyse Badiou's theoretical trajectory and development. An abstract continuity, in this case, secured by the biographical passage of the thinker through the heat of '68 and the frigid 70s, renders these early texts as the archival details over-determined by his present thinking. Despite my disagreement with Bosteels, it is on this point that we do obliquely share a common observation. He notes that, 'From "serving the people" to "serving truth" thus could sum up the trajectory behind Badiou's post-Maoism'.[11] This keen observation indeed highlights what I agree to be a break within Badiou's work that can be taken up as the key interpretive tool to open up his early writings.

The difference between 'serving the people' and 'serving truth' can be starkly underlined in his earlier work. Even in a cursory way, Badiou's early relationship with formal logic and mathematics was shot through with a political overtone that can be brought to sharp contrast with his later work around the time of *Being and Event*. A text such as the 1968,

11. Bosteels, 'Post-Maoism: Badiou and Politics', p. 584.

'*La Subversion Infinitésimale*' demonstrates Badiou's intent to bring class struggle within mathematics itself and to distinguish, through the Althusserian modes of the ideological and scientific, a divisionary critique within the history and development of the calculus and analysis itself. This articulation of a 'one divides into two' thesis may still be detected in Badiou's current dispositional preference for algebra over topology or set theory over analysis, but this preference is no longer in any sense inscribed within class struggle. One can also trace the stark difference between the *Concept of Model* and, say, *Number and Numbers* along these lines. I do not mean to over-emphasize Badiou's relationship with formalism to make this point. It does serve however to highlight the thematic importance that 'serving the people' played in his early work even when explicit continuity is present in terms of subject matter. In turn, Badiou's later treatments of conditions as distinct as art, through inaesthetics, political thought, through meta-politics, love, through psychoanalysis, will privilege the everywhere present orientation of *truth*. Indeed, what may immediately strike the reader in her first thumbing through the pages of *Rational Kernel* may be that this text, ostensibly about a philosophical topic, Hegel's dialectic, is precisely lacking in what will later dominate Badiou's philosophical rallying cry: the theme of truth.

It is indeed the reinvention of the concept of truth and Badiou placement of the theme at the centre of his philosophy that defines much of his current conceptual personae. It is also around the theme of truth that Badiou's philosophy achieves a systematicity unseen in his early work. Indeed, the entire theory of conditions, serving as the extra-philosophical contexts of conflicts and transformations, is ineffectual without its link to philosophy through the concept of truth. Borrowing equally from the Bachelardian-Althusserian notion of epistemological obstacle/break, the Sartrean dialectical use of nothingness, the Lacanian-Millerian configuration of the void-signifier relation, Badiou's late systematic articulation between philosophy and conditions envelops a depth that I cannot enter into here. What is most salient in my argument is the means by which Badiou weaves a systematic thought through the intimate relationship that the theory of conditions shares with a philosophy of truth.

In the most general terms, Badiou's system is invested in the connection between, on the one hand, local truths in politics, art, love and science and, on the other hand, philosophy itself. Indeed, this notion of truth is far from the conventional notions of veracity and reality. Tied to a dialectical understanding of the 'new' in history, truth is what breaks with sedimented and organized knowledge that reigns over a particular field and structures it. It is thus intrinsically local and singular, formed by the pressing impasses of a particular configuration of thought, as well as universal, in that it is expressed by its breaks with any particular configuration. The very constitution of a truth is generated by the unregimented concatenation of local investigations around this broken hiatus in knowledge. Post-Galilean science, for example, sought to reconstruct a consistent theory of motion for ordinary and heavenly bodies outside of the Aristotelian framework just as post-Newtonian physics encountered space and time outside of the conventions of fixed reference. In these cases, it is a subjective orientation toward hypothetical risk rather than a reliance of conventional 'veracity' that allowed the development of scientific truth. The evental emergence of the 'new' in each of the fields as well as the subjective carrying out of these local constructions provide the very means for philosophy's intervention. As Badiou explains, 'The specific role of philosophy is to propose a unified conceptual space in which naming *takes place* of events that serve as the point of departure for truth procedures. Philosophy seeks to gather together all the additional-names [...] It does not establish any truth but it sets a locus of truths'.[12] Indeed, in carrying out the name 'post-Galilean', subjective dices were thrown by the likes of Descartes, Huygens, Leibniz and Newton. In turn, a philosophical space was created such that scientific disputes poured into aesthetic, moral, political and metaphysical arguments which would characterize the transformation of early modern philosophy into the context of the Enlightenment. It is this sort of systematic connection that characterizes Badiou's vision of philosophy's role. On the one hand, there is a tremendous amount of activity everywhere: struggles in the political field, blind-spots in artistic experimentation, paradoxes in scientific processes, unique instances of people in love. These conditions are at once mixed, collective, solitary, intentional and contingent. Yet, out of this complex context of activities, an event emerges that breaks the standard modes of continuing on. The breaks that divide history provide the cracks from which new modes of thinking and acting concatenate to form a truth, in art, in science, in love and in politics. Philosophy in turn, provides a locus in which these truths are meditated upon, made compossible and register their universality despite their local and singular existence.

In brief, Badiou's systematic philosophy ties philosophy with the conditions of art, politics, love and science with the fragile but blisteringly

12. *Manifesto for Philosophy*, p. 37.

light of truth. In turn, the distinction between philosophy and these conditional domains, seen through the perspective of philosophy and *its* conditions, cannot either be maintained or related without the centrality of truth. While I cannot enter into the depth of Badiou's idiosyncratic account of truth here, I do wish to underline that his entry into a systematic vision of philosophy, characteristic of his later work, replete with a theory of conditions, is part and parcel with the centrality of truth itself as both extra-philosophical and orienting compass that directs philosophy to bottom-up actuality and non-particular universality. Insofar as it is the centrality of truth that systematizes a theory of condition, the lack of truth in his earlier works can be retroactively interpreted as a series of conditions without systematic organization, that is, without philosophy and thus without *locus*.

The lack of locus, the without-place of Badiou's early thought represented paradigmatically within the pages of *Rational Kernel* constitutes the very difficulty of the text. It is presented as a book *about* a philosophical nexus but not a philosophical book. Its page by page attempt at 'serving the people' through divisionary and critical readings strikes the readers familiar with Badiou's work as taking on an uncharacteristic external relationship to philosophy. Here, more than the lack of truth, Badiou forces us to encounter a strange voice.[13] Not only does Badiou equate truth with reality (albeit a dialectical notion of concrete reality) but philosophy is itself taken up, with Althusserian echoes to be sure, as a foreign and external object, subject to a criticism that aims only at division and intervention rather than universality, singularity and truth.

The attempt at division is the central aim of the book. Carrying out the imperative 'one divides into two', Badiou and his compatriots Mossot and Bellassen aimed to perform nothing short of this in their translation, annotation and introduction that comprise the present volume. This critical and divisionary project is characteristic of Badiou's early work and can be seen in ready action through a number of his published works throughout the 60s and 70s. Badiou's late drive toward

13. In the preface of the re-edition of Badiou's essays on Wittgenstein by the publishing house Nous in 2009, he underlines that, 'The philosopher assumes the voice of the master. Philosophers are not, nor can they be, modest participants in team work, laborious instructors of a closed history, democrats given over to public debates. Their word is authoritarian, as seductive as it is violent, committing others to follow suit, disturbing and converting them. Philosophers are present, as such, in that they state, even if this presence is also that of an exemplary submission, they do not subtract themselves from the duty of reason'. Alain Badiou, *Wittgenstein's Antiphilosophy*, trans. Bruno Bosteels, London, Verso, 2011, p. 68. See Alain Badiou, *L'Antiphilosophie de Wittgenstein*, Caen, Nous, 2009, p. 8.

philosophical systematicity may be deeply contrasted with the theme of division in this early work. At the same time however, it is the very ambiguous nature of division that will force Badiou's external approach to philosophy to encounter a space of thought that will later be occupied by the mantle of philosophy.

From a contemporary perspective, Badiou's explicit treatment of philosophical systematicity, the relation between truths, conditions and the event, is put forth through a critique that is simultaneously opposed to the historical developments within modern philosophy as well as the milieu of 'post-modernism' that dominated the period of his initial development of his systematic vision. While insisting on truths as extra-philosophical, the dangers of the identification of philosophy with these local truths produces a 'suture'. The suture of science and philosophy constitutes an identification of philosophical thought and scientific objectivity that is unfortunately typical of contemporary so-called 'analytic' philosophy. No doubt, the advent of the post-Galilean scientific condition impacted the orientation and development of modern philosophy in a deep and evident manner, an impact that understandably engendered the very sort of suture Badiou balks against. Yet, the over-identification of philosophical tasks with science itself signifies a veritable retreat from philosophy itself. At the same time, Marxism's suture of philosophy with proletarian politics casts philosophy as a mere 'epistemology of historical materialism'.[14] Here, we can underline that in Badiou's early works, where Althusser's epistemological task concerning historical materialism exacted a significant influence, there was a fundamental resistance to this sort of problematic suturing. As *Concept of Model* demonstrates, ideology and science remain distinct from philosophy itself and an invented space of reflexively mediates between the two. Despite writing a text addressed politically to comrades, Badiou's treatment of the dialectic in *Rational Kernel* also steers clear of any direct identification of philosophy with either science or ideology. Hence, although the Marxist-Leninist Badiou does not speak through the voice of the philosopher and despite treating philosophy externally as a complex locus of intersecting political, scientific and ideological debates, the temptation of the additional step of suturing philosophy to politics was consciously resisted.

With Badiou's later notion of philosophy as a 'locus of truths' in mind, we can understand the theoretical project of the *Rational Kernel* as one of locus. The problem of space is immediately evident. The text bridges

14. *Manifesto for Philosophy*, p. 64.

China and France. Taken as two contemporaneous loci of political struggle over the waning of the Leninist program, each of these geographical contexts is framed in terms of the interpretation of dialectics. In purely theoretical terms, the 'one divides into two' controversy in China was starkly different from that of Badiou's French context. Among the most important debates, the problem of the 'synthesized economic base' concerned the economic and industrial policy of China during the period of Sino-Soviet split.[15] The failed 'Great Leap Forward' and the withdrawal of Soviet intellectual and material capital pushed industrial development to the forefront of political confrontation. Faced with the urgency to respond to imperialist wars on all sides, the problem of 'one divides into two' concerned the very nature of the nascent socialist state and how it would mediate internal development, diplomacy and war. These concrete problems were no doubt expressed as intra-party struggle, the very roots of the GPCR. In this context, the inscription of the 'one divides into two' controversy as the general thematic of immense transformation of class composition, economic policy, factional disputes was a deliberate attempt to provide an ideological narrative to cast the multi-faceted problems of Chinese socialism, at that historical conjuncture, with a single expression. French Maoists, in their divergent forms, faced a starkly different political battle. The consolidation of European communist parties, the problem of revisionism and the new political formations constructed between students and industrial workers constituted a starkly different situation. Here too, Badiou and other Marxist-Leninist faced problems of a dialectical nature but a radically different material basis. It would be all too reductive and idealist to assert that the 'substance' of the Marxist-Leninist revolutionary party met its historical exhaustion in France (or Europe) and in China under different modalities. The intensive explosion of factional militancy within the GPCR is hardly equivalent with the sectarian dilution of new and increasingly minoritarian experiments

15. The philosophically invested debates that occupied the GPCR appear across a large number of different contexts. Among the venues that published philosophically charged writings, from the perspective of Mao's hegemonic perspective, during the heat of the GPCR were Renmin Ripao (People's Daily, the newspaper of record that continues to be so today), Hongqi (Red Flag, an important but now discontinued official journalistic and editorial outlet for the Chinese Communist Party) and Guangming Ribao (Enlightenment Daily). A number of the editorials have been published and translated into English in 1973 by Beijing's Foreign Languages Press as *Three Major Struggles on China's Philosophical Front.* It provides an overview of the controversy that 'one divides into two' had on the GPCR and addresses the problem of the 'synthesized economic base' in particular. See Revolutionary Mass Criticism Writing Group, *Three Major Struggles on China's Philosophical Front,* Beijing, Foreign Languages Press, 1973.

coupled with the feeble concentration of mainstream Communist parties. Despite Badiou's more recent assessments of the situation, within the pages of *Rational Kernel* as well as other texts during this period, a space of problematics was still operational and unity was sought not in the commonality of objective problems and positive projects but rather that of a shared context of negativity.

In *Rational Kernel*, Badiou appears keenly aware of the sharp distinction between the Maoism practiced by the Red Guards and his own context. Outside of the most abstract and polemic terms, there is no illusion of common struggle. This revolutionary sobriety is indeed a mark of his application of the 'one divides into two' slogan. Indeed, despite the differences between the Chinese and French contexts, some continuity pertinent to the party-form can be common-sensically underlined. Over and above all the pertinent analogies between the GPCR struggles concerning the party and the masses and the various French Maoist attacks on the ideological leaders of the French Communist Party, it was, for Badiou, the empty form of division that draws these different struggles together. Rather than slowly reconstructing a material account of concrete relation between the struggle in France and in China, philosophy served as a discourse, taken *in media res*, of an empty and nominal form of connection. Instead of pretending that the peeling away of the political layers of the 'one divides into two' controversy may reveal the unifying or originary conflict underlying the political malaise of Marxism, Badiou recognizes that the expression and its active dialectical kernel exists as an act that consists in its punctuality. Dialectics can only exist as the aleatory marker by which the very exercise of dialectics and its status division knots China and France together, not as a unity expressed differentially across geographical divide but as mutually reflecting mirrors of activity and pathology.

It is through a empty divisionary and negative gesture expressed throughout *Rational Kernel* as the concrete nature of the dialectic that Badiou knots together the themes as diverse as Lenin's reading of Hegel, the red guards' treatment of the dialectic, the 'New Philosophy' of Glucksmann, Althusser's materialism and Sartre. The voided space of dialectical division takes up 'philosophy' as the space of symptomatic conflict. Zhang Shi Ying's dialectical omnibus only serves to delineate the borders of this locus. Indeed understanding the thirteen alphabetically listed elements as a guiding thread in this diverse array of items from Hegel's *Logic*, we could read these interventions as the divisions within philosophy that are articulated *by* key conflicts within the GPCR. Each of these points constitutes the tracing of philosophy back to politics and attempts to open up the dialectical conflict at each stop. It is in this dialectical unpacking that each of these points also serves as the point where struggles in France and China are mirrored.

Though a common theoretical front in these different struggles is implied, this mirroring is far from a unifying gesture. Dialectical conflict allows us to identify points but not synthesize them into any resulting continuum. This very identification, here registered within philosophy, is arranged as a series of scissions. As Badiou forcefully argues in his annotation,

> The historical destiny of this [Hegelian] topology is its inevitable division. We can in effect conceive it in a purely structural fashion: exterior and interior are to be discernable *at each point*, but indiscernible in the supposedly given all.... This unity does not have any other evidence than its punctual effect, which is separation. The truth of the one is only insofar as it cannot be said *in whole* since the whole exists at each point as the act of a partition, of a two.[16]

The figure that recommends itself in this theoretical exposition is none other than the Moebius band.[17] Badiou explains that, 'In its global torsion, the ribbon does not admit to the distinction between interior and exterior. At each point, there is an 'inverse', thus an outside. As such, the all rematerializes as the scission interior/exterior, we need to cut the ribbon'.[18] A moebius band is a non-orientable (one-sided) surface and the 'difference', here understood as inside and outside, between the surfaces is a local appearance. The global nature of the band is a continuous singular surface where there is no such difference. Cutting along the centre of the band preserves the torsion and will produce, not two separate bands but a longer band with two twists. This sort of cut, an iteration that does not 'undo' the torsion of the original topos, may be analogized as the divisionary preservation of the torsion caught in the dialectic itself. Here, one does not divide into two and neither does two fuse into one. Rather, one divides into one. The cut that Badiou recommends in this passage,

---

16. Alain Badiou, *Le noyau rationnel de la dialectique hégélienne*, Paris, Maspero, 1978, p. 38-39 (below p. 58).

17. An important reference for Badiou's use of the moebius in relation to subjectivity and the 'cut' is no doubt Jacques Lacan's 'Science and Truth', first published in the first volume *Cahiers pour l'analyse*. See Jacques Lacan, 'Science and Truth', trans. Bruce Fink, *Newsletter of the Freudian Field*, vol. 3, 1988, pp. 4-29, p. 5.

18. *Le noyau rationnel de la dialectique hégélienne*, p. 39 (below p. 58).

across the band (perhaps more suited for the Gordian knot), is the destruction of torsion, a separation that divides the one into none.

The cut that is traced along the centre line of the Moebius band is indeed more suited as an analogy of what occurs in the *Rational Kernel*. The program of scission, of division, reproduces a continuous surface that undoubtably registers local torsion in increasingly more complex ways. With the act of division floating between contexts, the division of one into one extends the torsion: one divides into one. Within the text, the concatenated points, the division between France/China, Materialist/Idealist, *Phenomenology of Spirit/Science of Logic*, etc., are locally articulated as division. In turn, the divisionary split along these points continues to reproduce the global torsion. As Badiou is keenly aware only separation, the destruction of the torsion in the band, can count as true division. In one of the places in this text that employs the term 'truth', Badiou explains that, 'Truth is what has *no identity other than from a difference*; hence the being of all things is the process of its division into two'.[19] His use of the term here remains within a notion of truth as a Hegelian determinate reality. What is precisely ambiguous here is that Badiou uncomfortably straddles between two forms of division. On the one hand, the notion of identity as dialectical difference is more coherently schematized by the cut along the moebius band. From simple abstraction to complex concreteness, the cut along the band reveals the complexity of a global reality that is only apparently divided. On the other hand, the cut across the band, one that undoes the torsion, brings about a separation that utterly destroys the surface and renders a simple extended strip. As a division of the one into none, this separation unbinds any active problematic continuity.

Read retroactively from Badiou's current work, the earlier notion of truth as that which has no identity other than difference is replaced by the notion of being, the other, as it were, of truth. Untotalizable difference as identity itself, from the perspective of *Being and Event*, is precisely what is formalized by set theory. To compound our analogy, set theory can be said to be precisely what cuts along the moebius band, rendering a discourse of infinitely compounding and hierarchical differences. This amounts to the division of the one as inconsistent whole to one as the void. Alternatively, if we understand Badiou's divisionary project in *Rational Kernel* as expressing a proto-theory of conditions, then this concatenation of local conflicts globally united only by scission produces a

19. *Le noyau rationnel de la dialectique hégélienne*, p. 38 (below p. 60).

problem of locus. The empty formal act of division exhausts itself within the 'conditions' and identity ironically returns as the division that iteratively divides the one into one. Without the later systematic relationship in Badiou's thought between truth, condition and philosophy, the turbulent and conflictual torsions registered across discourses and acts would face the twin problems of exhaustion through differential division or destruction through a separation that disfigures any notion of condition. In turn, Badiou's use of philosophy in this text, regardless of its externalization, precisely provides the negative space that delimits the lack exercised by division.

To be clear, it is not the content of Zhang Shi Ying's philosophical work that, ostensibly aimed at elaborating dialectics as division rather than fusion, provides the space for Badiou's articulation of truth. It is rather the place that philosophy occupies within this arena of conditional differences that can be seen as a latent space where a locus was deemed necessary in order to register radical cuts. Zhang's work no doubt provides the perspective that allows the local mirrorings exercised within this text to be accomplished. Yet, within the later theory of conditions supplemented by a theory of truth, conditional divisions, cuts of separations, are given a locus where these divisions into two that occur contingently across regions of inconsistent multiplicity may be systematically registered. A locus that allows one to distinguish different cuts does not itself represent a higher unity of dialectical separation. Rather, it is only within a locus that distinctions between cuts, a one and a two, can be possible. In turn, it is only within the locus of philosophy that the counting of any 'two' or more confrontations with truth is possible. It is in this sense and not just any abstract relation secured between Badiou's Maoism and the later theory of conditions that a differential or evolutionary continuity between his earlier and recent thought can be established. In turn, it is only in Badiou's later works that the project of 'one divides into two', a theme that remained intensely unresolved in his early works, becomes accomplished. This accomplishment is none other than the separation between philosophy and truth, that is, the separation between philosophy as the register of divisions and the conditions as that which is divided. It is in this later context that the moebius band can be cut across and separation can effectively be registered within the thinking of compossiblity, universality and singularity.

To conclude, I wish to underline that my investigation in the above does not address the rich and varied content that traverses the text.

Starting from the perspective of the problems of the GPCR, the political conflicts within French Maoism and its relation to the proletarian movement in France, the transforming reception of Hegel within the European and Chinese context, Badiou's critique of structuralism, his relation to other contemporaneous philosophers and many other issues, intellectual historians and philosophers alike may draw insightful points from this compacted study that bridges a multitude of points. Bracketing this series of interests that the reader will no doubt discover between the covers of this book, my approach, far from comprehensive, situates itself from the starting observation of the lack of 'truth' in the text in question. As a term that is so intimately associated with Badiou's recent thought, its absence within this work indicates a site of excavation. In this approach, I have argued that it is not the morphisms of the dialectic but the evolution of Badiou's treatment of separation that allows us to create a theoretical continuity between this early work and his more recent contributions. In turn, I suggest that Badiou's later theory of conditions allows us a means to operate the reflexive relationship between a philosophy of truth and a history of truth. That is, if, for Badiou, philosophy is a locus wherein truth registers its divisionary and conflictual traces, then philosophy is itself a locus wherein local and conditional conflicts produces the marks that identify the actuality of the conditions and their transformation. Just as an active philosophical orientation pursues truths and registers evental sites with respect to their local conditions, such a perspective also allows us to work backwards, treating historical sequences from the perspective of the traces marked in philosophical work. It is precisely such an inverse conditional operation that takes place in *Rational Kernel* regarding the use of Hegelian dialectic in the political passage between May '68 to the bleak political landscape of the late 1970s. Of course, due to the directionality of this theoretical strategy, the need for the identification of a separate philosophical space, one that attempts to think divergent forms of division together in terms of actuality and compossibility, was muted. Along these very lines, if we, in turn, read this politically invested work from the perspective of his later philosophy, we find the opening of a political inquiry, a discrete moment of generic thought that takes up the difficult kernel of dialectics. Indeed, as the text demonstrates, dialectical division meets an impasse that remains insoluable with regards to the very problems that it engenders. In his next work, *Theory of the Subject*, Badiou will move strongly toward a systematicity that will attempt to think division through different subjective processes and thus begin to create a space where divisionary acts will constitute new continuities. It is through this intense reconfiguration of his thought that he will continue to refine his thinking of division. From separation to subtraction, it is only in the two volumes of *Being and Event* that one will finally be precisely and systematically divided into two, *and so on*.

Technical Note

A translation is by definition different from the original text but this translation most significantly differs from the original text in terms of the layout rather than content. In the original text, the commentary of Badiou et. al. on Zhang Shiying's text appears, as annotations often do, in the bottom margins of the page followed by yet another bottom margin of footnotes. For example, in the body of Zhang's text, they would insert 'Note D' which would then refer one to the note, at the bottom of the page, written by Badiou. These notes are of varying lengths and can either appear as a long footnote or at other times can split the page into two (which may be another sense of 'one divides into two'). At other times, the note overtakes the page completely. This layout may have the advantage of 'immediacy' and readers can see very clearly what Badiou was reacting to in Zhang's text in an instant. However, these un-uniform margins can also lead to confusion as to which text is on the page. In this edition, we have decided to put all the annotations as a separate section that begins after Zhang Shiying's text. Reading the text 'as it was intended' would require our readers to flip back and forth between Zhang's text and Badiou's commentary. For each note, we have provided the corresponding page number. Such a modification does change the immediate experience of the book but we believe this difference does not extend beyond this immediacy.

The Rational Kernel of the Hegelian Dialectic

The 'Yenan' Collection

Founded and run by organized Marxist-Leninist-Maoists, the 'Yenan' collection is an instrument of intervention in the theoretical and ideological conjuncture.

Drawn outside themselves by workers' power in May '68, the intelligentsia, decomposed and shattered have, since 1972, made a return.

To the anarchistic liquidators, who refused to 'save' Marx, even less Mao, putting an end to Lenin, the question of party and the dictatorship of the proletariat. To revisionists of all stripes, to sectarians of the ideologies of desire and their corresponding new academicism, to be more meticulous in the study and exegesis of texts so that they might refrain from taking sides, in thought as well as in practice, on what is of singular importance, the only thing which gives life and meaning to Marxist-Leninism: What is the meaning of the anti-revisionist battles in China and in Albania? What do we need to retain and transform to fight revisionism in France? What is, here and now, the path to follow for the fusion of Marxism and the real workers' movement?

The Yenan collection inscribes itself in the movement of these questions.

Three tasks:

1. Demonstrate that Marxism-Leninism is living, that only putting it into action permits the thinking of reality, the advancement in the theoretical domain, and the inscription in the camp of revolution.
2. Critique and denounce revisionism and its objective allies, the eclecticism of those which believe themselves to be able to dissect what they have announced as the cadaver of Marxism, for fabricating their 'new' theories, their fearful positivism, and their speculative syntheses, far away from class struggle, far away from history.

3. To attack the temporary hegemony of the new idealisms that supply the ideological elements of counter-revolution.

The Yenan collection is open to all those who share these three objectives.[1]

A. Badiou and S. Lazarus,
Directors of the collection

1. [This short foreword is followed by a list of current publications in the series, directed by A. Badiou and S. Lazarus. I have not reproduced the bibliography here but it includes Badiou's *Théorie de la contradiction*, *De l'idéologie* and Lazarus' *Eléments pour une théorie de l'Etat socialiste*.]

Foreword

This book undertakes the task of rendering explicit the question, which remains open, of the relation between Marxism and Hegel.

The two introductions ('Hegel in France' and 'Hegel in China') demonstrate the actuality of the question outside of all academicism. The core of the text is the translation of the book by Zhang Shiying, *The Philosophy of Hegel*, a book that engaged, in 1972, the philosophical struggles tied to the evaluation of the Cultural Revolution.

The notes, being of some length, are aimed at deploying the text of Zhang with regard to our own militant philosophical preoccupations. As such, their relative autonomy with respect to Zhang's argumentation are intended to designating what are, *for us*, the text's limits.

What follows is the list of the notes:

(a) On being, nothing, becoming: the Hegelian concept of contradiction and the problem of commencement
(b) On the interior and the exterior. Hegelian topology
(c) One divides into two
(d) On the sense of the word 'critique'
(e) On the category of negation
(f) On the laws of dialectic
(g) Quantity and Quality: place, excess, destruction
(h) History of Philosophy, real history, Glucksmann, Heidegger
(i) Class struggle on thought and being
(j) On the term 'active character' [*caractère agissant*]
(k) The philosophical concept of deviation
(l) 'In sticking close to the content' [*En collant de près au contenu*]
(m) Synthesis on the materialist dialectic

If you comrades here already know materialism and dialectics, I would like to advise you to supplement your knowledge by some study of their opposites, that is, idealism and metaphysics. You should read Kant and Hegel and Confucius and Chiang Kai-shek, which are all negative stuff. If you know nothing about idealism and metaphysics, if you have never waged any struggle against them, your materialism and dialectics will not be solid. The shortcoming of some of our Party members and intellectuals is precisely that they know too little about the negative stuff. Having read a few books by Marx, they just repeat what is in them and sound rather monotonous. Their speeches and articles are not convincing. If you don't study the negative stuff, you won't be able to refute it. Neither Marx nor Engels nor Lenin was like that. They made great efforts to learn and study all sorts of things, contemporary and past, and taught other people to do likewise. The three component parts of Marxism came into being in the course of their study of, as well as their struggle with, such bourgeois things as German classical philosophy, English classical political economy and French utopian socialism. In this respect Stalin was not as good. For instance, in his time, German classical idealist philosophy was described as a reaction on the part of the German aristocracy to the French revolution. This conclusion totally negates German classical idealist philosophy. Stalin negated German military science, alleging that it was no longer of any use and that books by Clausewitz should no longer be read since the Germans had been defeated.

(Mao Zedong, Talks at a conference of secretaries of provincial, municipal and autonomous region party committees, part II, January 1957[1])

1. [Mao Zedong, Talks at a conference of secretaries of provincial, municipal and autonomous region party committees, part II in *Selected Works of Mao Tse-Tung*, vol. 5, Foreign Languages Press, 1967, retrieved 1 December 2008, <http://marxists.org/reference/archive/mao/selected-works/volume-5/mswv5_57.htm>.]

Hegel in France

> Without German philosophy, particularly that of Hegel, German scientific Socialism (the only scientific Socialism extant) would never have come into existence.
>
> Engels, Preface to *The Peasant's War in Germany*, 1874[1]

The vitality of Hegel in France, other than the fact of its recent arrival, follows a singular trajectory which continues to obscure its rapport with Marxism and reactively undoes the rational kernel of dialectics.

It was in the seminar of Kojève in the thirties that one should date, in our opinion, a certain sort of inscription, not of a purely academic nature, of Hegelian references to the ideological questions of the time. From this moment on, an image of Hegel was sketched that took more than thirty years to undo—still, we are not far enough from it.

The Hegel of Kojève was exclusively that of the *Phenomenology of Spirit*, taken as the idealism of the scissions of self-consciousness, held in the ascending metaphor that follows from sensible immediacy to absolute knowledge, with, at its heart, the master-slave dialectic. It was the formalism of the encounter with the other that had the poetic virtue of placing itself under the sign of risk and death: this Hegel found its audience with the revolutionary romanticism of Malraux and even more with the surrealists. Bataille and Breton owed everything they said to Kojève.

Solidly founded on the translations and essays of J. Hyppolite, this unilateral figure proceeded after the war to a promotion of the masses

1. [Friedrich Engels, '"Preface" to "The Peasant War in Germany"', in *The Works of Friedrich Engels*, trans. Moissaye J. Olgin, International Publishers, retrieved 1 December 2008, <http://marxists.org/archive/marx/works/1850/peasant-war-germany/ch0b.htm>.]

under a Sartrian form. The pessimist doctrine of the 'for-others' [*pour-autrui*] (hell is other people) gave it support. On the psychoanalytic side, Lacan himself, remaining anchored to his friendship with the surrealists, in his early texts, found in it the elements for elaborating his doctrine of the imaginary: narcissism and aggressiveness were in symmetry with the master and the slave.

In brief: surrealists and existentialists found in Hegel something with which to forge an expansive romanticist idealism, in placing the affective subject at the heart of the experience of the world, its pathos measured up to the terrible historical thunder provoked everywhere by the effects of the Bolshevik revolution. With regards to the forms of consciousness of October 17, the crisis, the fascism, the war refigured as a storm, the young Hegel, the man who gave the final account of '89 and the Napoleonic wars, served as the siege machine against the dusty positivism of the national academies, against the sinister purr of French post-Kantians, against the secular humanism of the 'thinkers' of the radical party.

Hegel in France was, first of all, and above all, a tragic idealism against a scientific idealism. In this sense, its eruption is the disguised testimony of the times and substituting, in the most profound subjective ideals, the double figure of the cursed writer and the professional revolutionary of the 3rd international, of the world's most violent and secretive men [sic] with gentlemen decorated like the under-prefect [*sous-préfectorale*] of the member of the institute.

On this terrain, the encounter with Marxism was inevitable at the same time as it was impossible. Subjectively, the Hegelians of this period spoke of revolution while they looked forward to the order of the bourgeoisie. Breton and Sartre had to come to this obligatory crossing: becoming 'fellow travelers' with the communists. But insofar as being champions of romanticist individualism, like Malraux, they could not tolerate the mental consequences of accompanying their companions to the end. In the exemplary case of Sartre, who arrived at a time of ambiguity with respect to the proletarian reality of the party, this contradictory situation gave place to a gigantic enterprise, where there was, in a recurrent fashion, a multiple ancestry, notably in Germany: Marxism enters onto a stage of subjective idealism. Hegel returns this time, by a reversal of the Marxist reversal, as a tool for reversing dialectic materialism from head to toe. The entire history of a Hegelianized Marxism, for which the central category was alienation, plays on a key text of Marx: the *1844 Manuscripts*.

There again, the lesson of Kojève was not lost because it underlined the engendering, at the unleashing of the master-slave dialectic, of the category of labor, the focal point of the apparent fusion of Marxist political economy to the avatars of self-consciousness.

In *The Critique of Dialectical Reason* (but after the young Lukàcs, after Korsch), Sartre, in a similar move, hailed Marxism as the unsurpassable horizon of our culture and undertook the task of dismantling this Marxism in realigning its power with an idea of foreign origin: the transparence of the cogito. Such was, in truth, outside of the closed circle of party intellectuals who held themselves to a form of scientism in the style of Jules Guesde, the only Marx available to the French market, and at the same time, the only Hegel.

Both were false, this Marx and this Hegel, the first reduced to the second, and the second separated from the very part which had precisely led the way for the first: *The Science of Logic*.

The counter current was inevitable the moment when the historical horizon shifted at its base. The completion of the cycle of effects of the Second World War, the harsh setbacks of the revolutionary public of Soviet Russia, the PCF [*Parti Communiste Français*] clearly engaged in bourgeois and chauvinist revisionism (the experience of the Algerian war marks the decisive point), and, with the rising rigor of the Chinese proletarian, everyone was forced to take sides on the wars of national liberation, the intellectuals had to reinvent another ground to reclassify these distinct ideals. The 'fellow traveller' fell dead with malnutrition. He stopped having recourse to the philosophies of consciousness, whose role had been to preserve, with regards to a fascinating revolution, the double relation of engagement and 'to each his own'.

In solidarity for an instant, the intellectuals felt the constraint to identify themselves as such and to redefine their relation to Marxism from this basis. The first task given to this absolute valorization of knowledge and the intellect was structuralism. The second, by a violent upturn, made Marx, in lieu of being a metaphysician of the other and of work, a scholar of social structure. In both cases, we broke brutally with Hegel.

As we know, it was Althusser who pulled the trigger on the idealized Marxism of this later period, who discredited the young Marx of the 1844 manuscripts and made Hegel the absolute contrast, taking us to the thesis of a radical discontinuity between Hegel and Marx as the point on which everything becomes clear.

This work of housekeeping had its positive effects during this time, supported from far away by the assault of the Chinese against modern revisionism in the doctrinal form of the time. Althusser resituated in Marxism a sort of brutal edge, removed from the subjectivist tradition and remounted on the saddle as positive knowledge. At the same time, Marx and Hegel, despite being inverse terms, found themselves just as much foreclosed as during the previous period. For the second, as a unilateral figure, taken for a target, was treated with caution: the materialist Hegel of *The Science of Logic* was just as mute for Althusser as he was for Sartre. As for the first, suited to the concepts of structuralism, what was lost in the historicity of classes was not regained from science. The Hegelianized Marx of the fifties was a speculative figure but remained virtually revolutionary, while the anti-Hegelian Marx of the sixties was a scholar devoted to seminars. Or, to put the alternatives philosophically: the Marx-Hegel was the idealist dialectic, the anti-Hegel Marx was metaphysical materialism.

What the Cultural Revolution and May '68 tried to understand at the level of the masses was that we needed something other than the oscillation between the national intellectual traditions (between the Descartes of the *cogito*, Sartre, and the Descartes of the machine, Althusser) for reinvesting in a Marxism of real revolutionary movement. In the fierce storm, the positivist Marx of Althusser turned out to be more menacing, with its mingling with the 'scientific and technological revolution' of the PCF, than the idealist Marx of Sartre. We saw this clearly in their choices in crisis: Althusser on the side of Waldeck Rochet in the final count, and Sartre with the 'Maos' [the Maoists] despite all else.

It is certainly necessary today to establish in France what Lenin in 1921 (and à propos of the errors of Trotsky on syndicalism) called for, a vow to form: 'a sort of society of materialist friends of the Hegelian dialectic', to which he assigned the task of nothing less than a 'propaganda of the Hegelian dialectic'.

If there were any question of urgency, we can simply observe what the 'new philosophers' (nouveaux philosophes), with Glucksmann at the helm, are trying to do as they attempt to 'come full circle'.

During the first half of the century, Hegel served as an idealist mediation for the needs of our intelligentsia. This was followed by the revenge of the all powerful scientistic tradition: it was the apolitical Marx of the professors who has taken the scene; Hegel disappeared in the bitter backstage.

The Maoist proposal is to break this cycle, this counter-move. What do we find here? The 'new philosophers' dangle Hegelianism as a spectre, as the rational monster of the state. By the hatred aimed at dialectics, in reproaching Althusser, they have, rather than creating an effect of obscurity, shed more light on Marx, even as others sought to propose an embellishment of Marx and Hegel with new identities, in the sombre collections of the master thinkers from whom evil was unleashed.[2]

As such, for closing in on the process initiated in the thirties, this time, for acclimatizing ourselves to Marxism, and for our confession of its horror, we will again manipulate this sphinx at the centre of our philosophical thinking: the maintenance of the scission of the dialectic between Hegel and Marx.

In truth, we should begin again at zero, and to ultimately see, philosophically, that Marx is neither the same nor the other of Hegel. Marx is the divider [*diviseur*] of Hegel. He simultaneously assigns its irreversible validity (the rational kernel of the dialectic) and its integral falsity (the idealist system).

Hegel remains the stakes of an interminable conflict. Thus a working understanding of its division is the only one that forbids, in thinking the Marx/Hegel relation, not only the idealist-romanticist deviation, but the scientistic-academic deviation, and finally also the all-out hatred of Marxism.

The restitution of Hegel in his role is not in vain, since it is always either in the emblem of his exclusion or his entirety that the bourgeois philosophers *on the attack* operates, not in the ignorance of Marxism but in its study and in its neutralization.

It remains necessary to render speech to a gagged Hegel, to an essential Hegel, one on whom Lenin feverishly annotated, one from whom Marx had drawn the intelligence of the *Capital*: the Hegel of the *Logic*.

We are trying, we are beginning.

November 1977

2. [See André Glucksmann, *The Master Thinkers*, trans. Brian Pearce, New York, Harper and Row, 1980.]

Hegel in China

If Hegel as such did not constitute the content of the numerous debates which were unleashed in the philosophical front in China since 1949, it has often been the object of study or of particular re-examination. Other than numerous references to the Leninist reading of the author of the *Logic*, Mao Zedong mentions Hegel in *On Contradiction*, 'The famous German philosopher Hegel, who lived in the late 18th and early 19th centuries, made the most important contributions to dialectics, but his dialectics was idealist. It was not until Marx and Engels, the great protagonists of the proletarian movement, had synthesized the positive achievements in the history of human knowledge and, in particular, critically absorbed the rational elements of Hegelian dialectics...'.[1] In his *Talks at a conference of secretaries of provincial, municipal and autonomous region party committees* of 25 January 1957, Mao Zedong critiqued the total negation of classical German philosophy by Stalin, and insisted on the necessity of understanding the idealism and metaphysics for the better understanding of how to fight them, and to read 'Kant and Hegel and Confucius and Chiang Kai-shek'.[2]

The Hegelian philosopher was in any case historically interpellated from the concrete exigencies of the situation on the philosophical front. Before the liberation of 1949, a current of a rather 'classical' neo-Hegelianism dominated, one whose principle representatives was He Lin and from whom some major characteristics remain: a fear of the revolutionary essence of the dialectics; an accent put on the Hegelian theory of the state; a disinterest for the *Logic* and the importance accorded to the *Phenomenology of Spirit*, even a manic curiosity with respect to

1. [Mao Tse-Tung, '*De la contradiction*' in] *Oeuvres Choisies de Mao Tse-Tung*, tome 1, [Editions en langues étrangères], p. 252. [Mao Zedong, On Contradiction in *Selected Works of Mao Tse-Tung*, vol. 1, Foreign Languages Press, 1967, retrieved 1 December 2008, <http://marxists.org/reference/archive/mao/selected-works/volume-1/mswv1_17.htm>.]

2. [Mao, loc. cit.]

the structure of the *Logic* and the order of its concepts. After 1949, the field of discussion on Hegel had little by little constituted itself around the question of the usage of the Hegelian dialectic. Against those who made the relation between the dialectic, on the one hand, and idealism or materialism, on the other hand, as a relation of mere 'mechanic assemblage' [*assemblage méchanique*], a point of view that was affirmed with force: we should rather understand, through the internal contradiction of Hegel's philosophy, a contradiction between its conservative and revolutionary aspect, between an idealist system and the 'rational kernel'. Instead of understanding his dialectic as a totality, the dialectic divides into two. Another question raised by the Chinese: the end for which Hegel reserved for the law of the unity of contraries. He did not see it as constituting the core of the dialectic and had made the law of the 'negation of negation' the central element of the structure of his system, mechanically organizing the development at the interior of the chain 'thesis-antithesis-synthesis'.

The interventions on the philosophy of Hegel, the editions and re-editions of certain of his works since the establishment of the People's Republic of China groups principally around two periods:

-1956-1959: the months that preceded the Great Leap Forward of 1958 were punctuated by numerous appeals by Mao Zedong to massively study the dialectic and to practically understand its core, the unity of contraries. On the other hand, it was in the leading up to this period that the second great philosophical struggle was unleashed, on the identity of thought and being. In this context, in 1956, an important study entitled *On Hegel's Philosophy* was published by Zhang Shiying, who was, at the time, a professor in the department of philosophy of Beijing University. After this, in 1959, an important study entitled *On Hegel's Logic* was published by the same author; this text proposed to systematically examine and generalize, 'one of the most difficult texts of western philosophy' and, in a direct response to the grand authors of Marxist-Leninism, to continue the analysis and critique of the fundamental ideas of the *Logic*.

-1972-1975: The second period is marked by the consequences of the second plenum of the fourth congress of the Chinese Communist Party in august of 1970, in particular, by the directives of Mao Zedong on the study of the history of Chinese and Western philosophy and on the critique of the apriorist theory of genius. This started the first phase of the criticism of Lin Biao. Since 1973, many histories of western philosophy had been published and they had included major sections on the introduction of Hegel. *Hegel's Philosophy*, the new work of Zhang Shiying, which was published in 1972 is one which we have undertaken to translate a chapter. It serves, on the one hand as, 'a source for the study of Marx and Lenin by workers, peasants, soldiers, revolutionary cadres and revolutionary intellectuals', and on the other hand it is explicitly inscribed in 'the struggle against apriorism and the idealist conception of history' against the bourgeois thinkers who 'exalt the conservative aspect of Hegelian philosophy [...] or those who adopt an obscurantist attitude of distrust for the progressive vestiges of history'.

January 1978

The Rational Kernel of Hegel's Philosophy

Zhang Shiying

The idealist system of Hegel's Philosophy constitutes a conservative, even reactionary aspect of his philosophy. However, his idealist philosophy is traversed by something of great value: the dialectic of Hegel is the first, in the history of philosophy, to have developed, as complete as it was systematic, the idealist dialectic. In this, he gave an account of the fundamental characteristics with the help of an idealist point of view. Marx noted that, 'The mystification which dialectic suffers in Hegel's hands, by no means prevents him from being the first to present its general form of working in a comprehensive and conscious manner'.[1]

Hegel considered that the Absolute Spirit, Absolute Idea, resides in movement, in incessant transformation and development; in the existing movement and development of internal connections and reciprocal conditioning. Truth is concrete: development has its own laws; internal contradictions are their source of development. At the heart of development, a conversion of quantitative change to qualitative change operates. Knowledge is the process of the deepening and incessant concretization of the abstract toward the concrete; from the simple towards the complex.... These dialectical ideas are the progressive, revolutionary aspect of Hegel's philosophy.

1. *Le Capital*, postface à la 2e edition allemande, Editions sociales, p. 29. [Karl Marx, Afterword to the second German edition in *Capital*, Vol. 1, London, Penguin Classics, 1990, p. 103.]

I. The principle relative to movement and the independence of phenomena

Hegel held that reality, truth, that is to say, what he called Absolute Spirit, the Absolute Idea, is a process of movement, transformation and incessant development. Each stage, each aspect or link of this process is not fixed or isolated. Instead, there exists internal relations and living conversions between them: the one converts itself, passes necessarily to an other and necessarily brings about profound interconnections.

Engels noted that,

> In this system—and herein is its great merit—for the first time the whole world, [the] natural, historical, intellectual, is represented as a process, i.e., as in constant motion, change, transformation, development; and the attempt is made to trace out the internal connection that makes a continuous whole of all this movement and development[2]
>
> Hegel puts forward two basic requirements:
> 1. 'The necessity of connection'
> and
> 2. 'the immanent emergence of distinctions'.
> Very important!! This is what it means, in my opinion:
> 1. *Necessary* connection, the objective connection of all the aspects, forces, tendencies, etc., of the given sphere of phenomena;
> 2. The 'immanent *emergence* of distinctions'—the inner objective logic of evolution and of the struggle of the differences, polarity'.[3]

2. Friedrich Engels, *Anti-Düring*, Editions sociales, p. 55. [Friedrich Engels, 'General Introduction', in *Anti-Düring*, Progress Publishers, 1947, retrieved 1 December 2008, <http://marxists.org/archive/marx/works/1877/anti-duhring/introduction.htm>.]

3. V. I. Lenin, *Oeuvres completes*, Editions de Moscou, t. XXXVIII; 'Science de la Logique de Hegel', p. 95. [V.I. Lenin, *Introduction in Conspectus of Hegel's Science of Logic*, Progress Publishers, 1976, retrieved 1 December 2008, <http://marxists.org/archive/lenin/works/1914/cons-logic/preface.htm>. Lenin's commentary here corresponds to p. 55 of A.V. Miller's translation of Hegel's introduction of Hegel's Science of Logic. G. W. F. Hegel, *Science of Logic*, trans. A.V. Miller, Amherst, Humanity books, 1999, p. 55.]

These two passages from Engels and Lenin are in reality a succinct generalization of the dialectical thinking of Hegel. From this, we can see that the dialectical thought of Hegel, from the point of view of its most important content, is a thought of the internal relation and development of contradictions. Lenin indicated that the 'differences', the 'polarity', are contradiction. Hegel himself said that, the only understanding, the only reality (that is to say, Absolute Spirit or Absolute Idea), that philosophy should master and understand fall under two characteristics: these are the two principles of development and of the concrete. These two characteristics are mutually related. More than this, Hegel undertook their synthesis; he gave a definition for what he called truth or reality. He said, 'Thus the Idea as concrete in itself, and self-developing, is an organic system and a totality which contains a multitude of stages and of moments in development'.[4] The concrete in question here designates the sum of the organic relations of different sorts where, according to the same expression of Hegel, make up 'the union of different determinations'.[5] Hegel himself used an example for explaining the meaning of 'concrete': a bouquet of flowers is comprised of its different qualities, such as its smell, its shape, its colour, however, the bouquet of flowers is not the fortuitous gathering of these qualities; it is a unity [*ensemble*]. In a bouquet of flowers, these qualities are related to one another in an internal and necessary manner. The abstract that we ordinarily speak of is opposed to this concrete. That is why, in saying that this bouquet of flowers is concrete, we mean to say that it is a unity that connects these qualities in an internal way. On the contrary, if one abstracts away a particular quality from this bouquet of flowers, like colour, one separates it from the other qualities and colour would then become abstract. In short, the concrete is the internal relations, it is the unity. The abstract is the separation, the unilateral. Hegel considered the things of the world concrete; they are unities in different aspects, elements or qualities related in an internal way. Whether it is in the heavens or on earth, in the natural or spiritual world, there is nothing 'abstract' or isolated; if one isolates something in an absolute way, it would be without sense. For example, a colour absolutely isolated, abstract, outside of all form, all smell, and all quality, does not exist in reality. In the real world, if a colour is not tied to such a shape,

---

4. Hegel, *Leçons d'histoire de la philosophie*. [G.W.F. Hegel, 'Introduction', in *Lectures on the History of Philosophy*, trans. E.S. Haldane, Lincoln, University of Nebraska Press, 1995, retrieved 1 December 2008, <http://marxists.org/reference/archive/hegel/works/hp/hpintroa.htm>.]

5. Hegel, *Leçons d'histoire de la philosophie*. [Hegel, *Lectures on the History of Philosophy*.]

such a smell, it would then be with another shape, another smell.... To put it simply, this is what Hegel means when he says that truth is concrete.

The second fundamental characteristic of truth is development. Hegel considered that, since truth is a varied organic unity, it also carries in itself certain contradictory elements, opposed elements, contradictions. This is why reality is not necessarily fixed or at rest, but can convert and contradictorily self-develop. Precisely because of this, Hegel added that truth is living; it is a movement and a process.

Hegel affirmed that the object of philosophy is truth-reality, having the characteristics outlined above, such that the sole goal of philosophy is to understand this truth, this reality. This is why Hegel considered 'philosophy as the apprehension of the development of the concrete'.[6] It is science that understands this truth-reality. From this fundamental point of view, we can say that the content of the entire Hegelian philosophical system is the description of the process of the development of the concrete truth-reality. This is the description of the process of deduction and the reciprocal conversion of each stage, each link contained in concrete truth or reality. Let us take, for example, the first part of the Hegelian philosophical system, the logic. The fundamental spirit which traverses the description of logical concepts consists in examining them as reciprocally linked things, in development and in incessant conversion. For example, when Hegel analyses the two concepts of Being and Nothing, we see that Being is not a fixed or ultimate thing: it has to pass and to convert itself into the opposing Nothing. As such, a purely abstract Being is, on the one hand, a different concept, opposed to the Nothing, but on the other hand, a purely abstract Being has no determinations and no content; what then would its difference be with the Nothing? Also, we cannot, as it is done in metaphysics, consider that Being is Being and Nothing is Nothing and that, between the two, there is absolutely no communication. On the contrary, Being and Nothing are tied in an internal and necessary way; the former in self-development converts itself into the latter [NOTE A, see below p. 51].

Another example, the two concepts of Freedom and Necessity: they are not entirely cut off or separated from each other. If one considers that, to be free, it suffices not to be determined by necessity or, on the contrary, to not be free, it suffices to be determined by necessity, we should say that this point of view has not considered the problem by leaving aside the issue of connections: it opposes liberty and necessity abstractly

6. Hegel, *Leçons d'histoire de la philosophie*. [Hegel, *Lectures on the History of Philosophy*.]

and is thus in error. A freedom that does not include necessity in itself, or does not act through the function of necessity is nothing but a 'formal freedom'. One cannot but call it arbitrary and it is hence not true freedom. Freedom is essentially concrete, that is to say that it is strictly tied to necessity: it is the understanding of necessity. Only such a freedom is true freedom. Another example: Essence and Phenomena. Hegel noted: Essence and Phenomena do not exist isolated from each other. Phenomenon is the manifestation of Essence; if a phenomenon is such a way, it is due to its Essence; further, Essence does not exist outside of Phenomenon but rather in it. Otherwise put, in what phenomena manifest, there is nothing that is not interior to Essence, and there is nothing in Essence that is not manifest in phenomenon. Outside of Essence, there is no manifestation of this Essence, there are no phenomena. Outside of phenomena, Essence becomes an empty thing which has no sense. This is why, in order to understand Essence, we need to begin with the understanding of phenomena. The separation of Essence and phenomena, in going outside of phenomena to apprehend an abstract essence, an unknowable thing-in-itself, this is the metaphysical perspective that Hegel critiques. [NOTE B, see below p. 58] Further, we can also take the general, the particular and the individual as examples. Hegel considered these to be the three links of the concept which are inseparable and tied in an internal fashion. On the one hand, the particular cannot exist outside of the general, the general structures the nature and the essence of the particular. However, the general is also inseparable from the particular: it manifests itself through the latter, it traverses the latter, the general comprises itself through the particular, it has the particular as content. All generality seized outside of the particular is empty and not real. Strictly tied to the particular, this generality is called 'the concrete generality' by Hegel and the cut-off generality of the particular is called 'the abstract generality'. Hegel is for the former and opposes the later. What he will call 'individuality' is the union of the general and the particular.

In brief, the concepts and categories that Hegel examines in the *Logic* (Being, nothing, becoming, quantity, quality, degree, essence, identity, difference, contradiction, essence and phenomenon, necessity and contingency, possibility and reality...) are found in a constant movement, are intertwined, and are mutually converting; they transform and develop one another, there is a conversion of the one into the other. This is why we might say that the logic describes the process of movement, conversion, deduction and the incessant development of the concept.

We have done nothing here but take some examples from the *Logic*, but, certainly, Hegelian thought on connection and development is not limited to this work.

The method of metaphysical thought considers things as immutable and without intertwining internal connections. Hegel has very vividly critiqued this conception. He has indicated that the metaphysical method does not carry out and does not understand that, truth-reality is concrete and has multiple aspects; it takes the abstract and isolated concept as being able to express truth, it always seizes on an aspect of things and does not let it go while thinking that it has delivered the whole truth. When it examines something, it never wishes to give attention to the other and opposed aspects; the aspect that is seized is never reconnected with the others. This method misunderstands the organic unity of the aspects of truth, it often expresses many diverse superficial phenomena of a problem but it never truly understands the treatment of the essence from the grounds of its organic unity. This method is arbitrary, operating through opinion, it takes up an aspect and considers that every aspect can exist in a state of isolation; it considers that between such and such an aspect there is an unbridgeable barrier, without any conversion or reciprocal transformation. As such, Freedom and Necessity, Essence and Phenomenon, Possibility and Actuality, Necessity and Contingency, all these concepts are cut off from one another as mutually exclusive. Hegel argues that a method of unilateral thought such as metaphysics cannot understand truth-reality.

II. The fundamental principle of dialectics (Contradiction)

The two characteristics of truth-reality laid out in the above already contain the idea of contradiction in themselves. Outside of contradiction, there is no question of the concrete or development. Hegel argued that if truth-reality is in movement, in transformation, in development, it is not because of an exterior force but rather due to an internal contradiction. He affirmed that, at each stage, each link of the process of development of the Absolute Spirit, of the Absolute Idea, carries within itself internal contradictions. According to the example that he himself takes up, the phenomenon of life contains the contradiction between life and death. The metaphysical perspective argues that, since life is different from death, they are mutually opposed; there cannot be factors of death in the phenomenon of life. According to this point of view, if man should die, it is uniquely because of external causes. Hegel has indicated that life is a contradictory process, 'The living dies, simply because as living they bear in themselves the germ of death'.[7] Since man cannot escape death, there is then, fundamentally, an internal cause. When there is a passage between the two, the conversion of a concept towards another, as Hegel describes in the *Logic*, it is not due to an external cause, rather a concept comprises the elements of another concept in nature and at the very interior of a concept which is (or are) opposed and different. It is for no other reason than an internal contradiction of the two aspects forced by the concept to convert and to pass into another concept. This process of conversion, movement and development of concepts described by the *Logic* in its entirely is also the process of auto-conversion, auto-movement and the auto-development of concepts. For example, if the concept of Being converts itself to the concept of Nothing, it is not because of an exterior force acting without internal interconnections with being, existing outside of being, that pushes it towards the conversion to the nothing, but rather because of the nature of this purely abstract Being, still without content, already carries the elements of this Nothing in contradiction.

7. Hegel, *Encyclopédie*, Vrin, p. 513. [Hegel, *Logic*, trans. William Wallace, Oxford, Oxford University Press, 1975, § 92 A]

The same goes for the concepts of Identity and Difference, Essence and Phenomena, Necessity and Contingency, Possibility and Actuality: the source of their reciprocal conversion also resides in internal contradiction. For example, if identity converts itself into difference, this is not because of an exterior force which has no internal links in germination, but rather because the concept of concrete identity holds in itself the concept of difference in contradiction. It is for no other reason than the internal contradiction between two aspects that the concept of identity is forced to overcome itself and to convert itself into the concept of difference. [NOTE C, see below p. 60]

The same goes for the other concept and categories. In brief, in all concepts and categories, in all phenomena—otherwise put, at each stage of the link of reality or absolute spirit—there are internal contradictions, and, in this, each overcomes itself and passes into its contrary. Metaphysics considers contradictions as unthinkable or at least illegitimate [*pas normales*]. Hegel critiqued [NOTE D, see below p. 61] this metaphysical conception. According to this point of view, the principle of contradiction in formal logic does not permit us to affirm something while denying it; it is the elementary law that our thought should respect. If thought infringed upon this law of formal logic, it would mean that it is not 'legitimate' [*pas normal*] it is 'unthinkable'. However, to understand the principle of contradiction in formal logic is not equivalent to rejecting the contradictions that exist in reality. Hegel affirms that in reality all concrete things are contradictory and, between heaven and earth, there is nothing that does not include contradictions or contrary characteristics. Hegel considered the contradictions that we speak of in the law of contradiction in formal logic as 'formal', they are 'impossible' contradictions and should be excluded. But real contradictions are absolutely different from what the principle of non-contradiction of formal logic would exclude. This type of contradiction is a necessary contradiction, one that is, 'internal' and for which, 'it is ridiculous to say that contradiction is unthinkable'.[8] Not only is this type of contradiction not an abnormal phenomenon, but it is 'the very moving principle of the world.'[9] It is 'the universal and irresistible power before which nothing can stay, however secure and stable it may deem itself'.[10] This is why, wherever there is

8. Hegel, *Encyclopédie*, p. 555. [Hegel, *Logic*, § 119 A2.]

9. [Hegel, *Logic*, § 119 A2.]

10. Hegel, *Encyclopédie*, p. 515. [The authors of the text seem to have given the wrong citation. Hegel, *Logic*, § 81 A1.]

contradiction, there is movement and development. Hegel railed against those who rejected contradictory things: 'the usual tenderness for things, whose only care is that they do not contradict themselves, forgets here as elsewhere that in this way the contradiction is not resolved but merely shifted elsewhere'[11]

Lenin indicated, 'This irony is exquisite! "Tenderness" for nature and history (among the philistines)—the endeavour to cleanse them from contradictions and struggle'.[12]

11. Hegel, *Science de la logique*, Aubier Montaigne, T. II, p. 57. [Hegel, *Science of Logic*, p. 423.] This is taken up in Lenin XXXVIII p. 129. [Lenin, *Conspectus of Hegel's Science of Logic*, retrieved 1 December 2008, <http://marxists.org/archive/lenin/works/1914/cons-logic/ch02.htm>.]

12. [Lenin, *Conspectus of Hegel's Science of Logic*.]

III. The principle according to which there is a conversion of quantitative change into radical qualitative change [NOTE F, see below p. 64]

Truth-reality develops, and from Hegel's point of view, this development is not only quantitative but qualitative; in effect, in the chapter on Being in the *Logic*, Hegel studied the laws of reciprocal conversion, the reciprocal relations between quantitative change and qualitative change. Hegel argued that quality and quantity are characteristics that ranged over everything. But there is a difference between quality and quantity. To summarize Hegel's own terms, quality is an inherent character in being while quantity does not directly apply. By the unity of quality and Being, Hegel means that quality is the determination that makes a thing a thing. A thing is what it is by its quality; if it loses its quality, it ceases to be such a thing. If there is such a quality, such a thing is; if there isn't such a quality, such a thing is not. As such, he concludes that quality is in unity with Being. To say that quantity is not directly unified with Being, this signifies that the greatness or the augmentation and diminution of quantity do not influence the quality of something, it does not influence whether it is or is not; the relationship between quantity and Being are external. [NOTE G, see below p. 66] However, while indicating the difference between quality and quantity, Hegel nonetheless underlines the close ties between the one and the other. For Hegel, the non-influence of quantitative change on quality holds only within certain limits. For example, regardless of the augmentation or the diminution of the temperature of water, it does not influence the nature of water itself. The same goes for the farmer who piles on the weight on his donkey: within certain limits, this does not influence the movement of the donkey. However, when the quantitative loading goes beyond the limit, it can bring change to one quality or another. Thus, if the quantitative rise of the temperature of water rises beyond certain limits, water becomes vapour; if it falls beyond certain limits, it becomes ice. All the same, if the farmer adds kilo after kilo on his donkey such that the burden mounts beyond certain limits, the donkey falls, unable to support the weight of the burden. Hegel underlined that we should not take these examples as jokes, because they are actually rich in meaning. These examples illustrate the law of conversion between quantitative and qualitative change in a lively fashion. They show that, at the start, quantitative change is without consequence from the point of view of quality, but when this change reaches a certain degree, it leads to a transformation of quality. Hegel indicated that quantitative change is a gradual and progressive movement; qualitative change is a rupture in gradation. Here Hegel clearly demonstrates the idea of development by leaps, and attacks the metaphysical perspective in which movement is reduced to a pure quantitative change.

IV. The principle according to which knowledge is a process that goes from the abstract to the concrete, from the simple to the complex

The concrete that is in question here, we have already said in the above, designates a varying unity. Hegel considered the process of development of truth-reality, that is to say, Absolute Spirit, the Absolute Idea, as being at the same time the process of its self-knowing. He considered the process of knowledge as a process that goes from the abstract, the superficial, and the poor, toward the concrete, the profound, and the rich. That is why the whole process of absolute spirit, from its logical stage to the spiritual stage by its passage through the natural stage, is a process that becomes more and more concrete, and more and more complex: 'the knowledge of mind is the highest and hardest, just because it is the most "concrete" of the sciences'.[13] We will now discuss this with more precision by taking logic as an example. Hegel considered the movement of each concept, of each category in logic as a function of internal contradiction. Each concept holds within itself, its own contradiction, and, as this aspect of negation is in contradiction with itself, it is finally refuted and converts itself into another concept, another category. However, the sense Hegel gives to negation is not the metaphysical conception of negation, or simple overcoming. It is a question of overcoming the primitive given in conserving what is rational. This is why the term of negation has, at once, a sense of termination and conservation. It is for precisely this that the process of knowledge, the process of conversion and the deduction of concepts that Hegel speaks of is not a process of overcoming a concept for another, but a process of deepening, a progressive concretization and an incessant enrichment of content. For example, in logic, the starting concept, Being, has absolutely no determination, it is the most abstract and empty concept. Yet, in traversing the process of negation, Being converts itself into becoming and then again into quality. Of course, the concept of quality is more concrete, more profound and richer, compared to simple Being.

13. Hegel, no doubt, in a hard to find section of the *Encyclopédie*. [G.W.F. Hegel, *Philosophy of Mind*, trans. William Wallace, Oxford, Oxford University of Press, 1971, p. 1.]

It thus expresses the idea that it comprises certain determinations that simple Being did not comprise. The same goes for the concept of degree: it is the last concept in the chapter on Being in the *Logic* and at the same time it is the richest and most concrete concept of this chapter because it does not only overcome the concepts of Quality and Quantity that preceded it, but comprises the two within it. It is the unity of Quality and Quantity. The same for the chapter on Essence: Reality [Actuality] is the last concept, it is at the same time the richer and the more concrete and it does not only overcome essence and phenomenon, it is the unity of the two. The same goes for the last concept of the last chapter of the *Logic*: the Concept, that is to say, the Absolute Idea, is the richest and most concrete of the whole of the *Logic*. It does not only overcome all the concepts and categories that precede it but it comprises everything in it. It is the unity of Being and Essence. All concepts and categories that precede it make up an integral part of it, as the links that constitute it. This is why the many parts of Hegel's logic are not simply the juxtaposition and the alignment of several concepts situated on an equal level, but actually different stages in a process of self-development, of self-knowing of the Absolute Idea. The definition of the Absolute Idea given here is the most abstract and superficial. Or, as it were, the knowledge that the Absolute Idea has of itself is the most abstract and empty. The concept of Essence is also not outside of the Absolute Idea, for, in reality, Essence is the Absolute Idea, but a rather inferior and less concrete stage of the Absolute Idea. The Absolute Idea is thus also Essence, but the definition that we have given for it is not very concrete, as it were, where the knowledge that the Absolute Idea has of itself is not very concrete. This is why the Absolute Idea is a great gathering of all its preceding concepts, and all these concepts are, in each one, stages of its self-development and at the same time its content. Outside of these stages, the Absolute Idea itself cannot but be empty and devoid of sense. This is why Hegel argued that in order to understand the Absolute Idea, it is necessary to understand each of the stages of its self-development. In order to understand the categories and ultimate and supreme concepts of logic, it is necessary to understand the whole system of its concepts.

We can thus see that the process of idea's self-knowledge in Hegel goes from the most abstract, superficial Being to traversing the process of a series of negations, passing from the stage of Being to the stage of Essence, and then from the stage of Essence to the stage of the Concept in order to finally stop at the Absolute Idea. The set of processes is the process of deepening and a progressive concretization of the abstract towards the concrete, going from the simple to the complex: in this process, each category is relatively superior and more concrete, more profound that the preceding categories. For expressing this idea, we can take yet another particularly clear example: the conception of history in Hegel's philosophy. Hegel considered philosophy as the supreme form of the Absolute Idea. That is why the history of the development of philosophy follows a path that goes from the abstract to the concrete and from the simple to the complex. Hegel was strongly opposed to the idea of the history of philosophy as a conglomeration or an alignment of disordered opinions. It is inapt and superficial to conceive of the metaphysical schools in the history of philosophy as excluding and annihilating one another reciprocally, that a metaphysical system 'kills' another metaphysical system, throwing it out as if a metaphysical system were dead and no longer has value. For Hegel, if the philosophical systems in the history of philosophy did take the stage at previous times, if there were not some links between these systems of philosophy, they would not have had any content. If a system of philosophy could exist, it is, as far as the grounds are concerned, because all philosophical systems appear necessarily and develops from preceding philosophical thoughts.

Hegel held that there is only one truth. Philosophy is auto-philosophy, self-knowledge and the self-knowing of truth. Each philosophical system has this single truth as its content and is thus a particular stage in the self-development and the self-knowledge of truth. The first philosophical systems were the most abstract and poor. In these philosophical systems, we find the development of truth at an inferior stage; the content and the determinations of truth were still extremely abstract and poor. Then, the more recent the system of philosophy, the more it masters truth in a concrete and profound way. At each superior stage, the more the content is concrete, rich and profound, the more we find truth. These recent philosophical systems have made these preceding philosophical systems their real existing materials. In taking these for their point of departure, they have reworked and transformed them; the recent philosophical systems have thus not simply rejected all the preceding philosophical systems but have utilized them for enriching themselves, they have made them their links and constitutive elements. Thus they conserve them in overcoming them. This is why the most recent and newest philosophies are more concrete, richer and more profound; they are a 'mirror of the whole history'.[14]

14. Hegel, *Leçons d'histoire de la philosophie* [Hegel, *Lectures on the History of Philosophy*.]

Hegel thus argued that for understanding the last form, that is to say, the latest current in the development of philosophy, we should understand the history of its past developments. The study of the history of philosophy is the study of philosophy itself. [NOTE H, see below p. 68]

Hegel's idea that thought is a process of the abstract towards the concrete and of the simple towards the complex can be expressed in the following fashion: reality is concrete; it is the unity of plural determinations. However, truth does not reach this concrete except by having traversed a long process of development. The first stage of self-development and self-knowledge of truth is the most abstract, that which lacks the most content, its determinations are the most simple. Then, after the incessant pursuit of the self-development and self-knowledge of truth, these determinations or particularities become more and more rich; the content is thus more and more concrete, and so forth until it reaches its final form. At this moment, all the determinations or the preceding particularities become its constitutive elements, its indispensable and inherent content; they are comprised within it. Here, truth reaches its supreme and ultimate stage, that is to say the most concrete and richest stage. The idea that knowledge is a process that goes from the most abstract towards the concrete, from the simple to the complex, is expressed by Hegel clearly in this passage: 'cognition rolls onwards from content to content. First of all, this advance is determined as beginning from simple determinatenesses the succeeding ones becoming ever richer and more concrete. For the result contains its beginning and its course has enriched it by a fresh determinateness. The universal constitutes the foundation; the advance is therefore not to be taken as a flowing from one other to the next other. In the absolute method the Notion maintains itself in its otherness, the universal in its particularization, in judgement and reality; at each stage of its further determination it raises the entire mass of its preceding content, and by its dialectical advance it not only does not lose anything or leave anything behind, but carries along with it all it has gained, and inwardly enriches and consolidates itself'.[15]

In the *Philosophical Notebooks*, Lenin greatly approved of these passages. He says: 'This extract is not at all bad as a kind of summing up of dialectics'.[16]

---

15. This citation is taken from Lenin, *Oeuvres complètes*, t. XXXVIII, 'Notes philosophiques'. [Lenin, *Conspectus of Hegel's Science of Logic*, retrieved 1 December 2008, <http://marxists.org/archive/lenin/works/1914/cons-logic/ch03.htm>. Cf. Hegel, *Science of Logic*, p. 840.]

16. [Lenin, *Conspectus of Hegel's Science of Logic*.]

Here, we can see Hegel's rational kernel through what concerns knowledge as a process of the abstract to the concrete and the simple towards the complex: concrete things in objective reality are precisely the reciprocal connection and the sum of multiple aspects; they are organic unities having plural determinations and varied aspects. In order to really understand a thing, it is necessary to master these connections of organic unity between all these aspects. However, in the process of real knowledge, humanity cannot master all at once the organic unity of all these determinations of concrete things. The process of knowledge that humanity has of the concrete character of things, the process of knowing the organic connection of all these aspects of a concrete thing is long and winding. The goal of mastering these things is not reached without passing through the process of an 'abstract activity'. What is called here an 'abstract activity' is the act of extracting one aspect, one determination from a whole and to understand it in isolation. To take up Marx's example from Introduction to *A Contribution to the Critique of Political Economy*, the population is a concrete thing, it is an organic unity of many aspects, many determinations. But when we understand a population, we do not have any understanding of the different elements that constitute the population at the start; we only have a chaotic conception.[17] So as to allow our knowledge to reach its goal, which is to master a concrete thing, the unity of plural determinations that is population, we should undertake these 'abstract activities', and analyse these 'chaotic conceptions' of population, analyse all the elements and determinations that constitute the population: for example, we examine the classes from the elements and determinations that constitute it, like wage labour, capital, and further we examine these elements to the point of all the elements and determinations that constitute waged labour and capital like exchange, the division of work, price... We should extract, with an increasing precision, the simplest elements and the determinations united in their origin in this concrete thing which is the population with the goal of knowing it. Yet, if one stops at the stage of 'abstract activity', we cannot then reach the stated goal of mastering the concrete thing. What we obtain at this stage is nothing but something abstract. The population is not at all a random gathering of elements and determinations such as class, waged labour, capital, etc. The population is always an organic unity of these elements and determinations. Also, for understanding concrete things, we should have a unified comprehension

17. [Cf. Karl Marx, *Grundrisse*, trans. Martin Nicolaus, London, Penguin Classics, 1973, p. 100-108.]

of these elements and simple determinations, understanding the relations and the organic unity between these elements and determinations. It is with this sole condition that we can know the true face of the population, its rich contents and thus say that we have achieved a concrete understanding. From this example, we clearly see that the process described by Hegel, a process that goes from the abstract to the concrete, from the simple towards the complex, reflects, in effect, in an unconscious manner, the process of real knowledge. Such is precisely the rational kernel of Hegel's conception.

V. The principle relative to the identity of thought and of being and the coincidence between the logical and the historical

An important principle of Hegelian philosophy is the identity between thinking and being. [NOTE I, see below p. 72] Kant considered there to be an unbridgeable trench between thinking and being and that the true face of being (the 'thing-in-itself') is something that thinking or knowledge can never reach: it is something that is by principle unknowable. Hegel critiqued this point of view. He opposed the metaphysical rupture between thinking and being; he considered that if we were to radically separate thinking and the thing itself (being) and if we were to affirm absolute separation of the thing itself and knowledge, then we would always be reduced to a state of not being able to know things and we would never be able to resolve the question of how knowledge is possible. Hegel says that this point to view drives us towards doubt and despair. Hegel advances the idea that the true aspect of a phenomenon, or a thing, is necessarily what is known to us through correct thinking and thus things-in-themselves are knowable in principle. Hegel considered that the two contrary aspects of thinking and being are united in an internal fashion: on the one hand, being is the content of thought. Without being, thought would lack content, since it would be empty. On the other side, outside of thought, things or being would lose their dimension of truth. Thought is what seizes and brings about the essence of things. For Hegel, things are nothing but the exterior manifestation or the 'exteriorization' of thought. Further, what is 'exteriorized' is finally brought to be negated and to re-entwined with its primitive base—to the interior of thought -this is why thought and being are in reality two aspects of the same thing. However these two aspects are not situated on the same footing, such that, according to Hegel's perspective, thought is what leads, it is first, it is then followed by things, or being, as subordinate; they are the products of thought.

On the basis of this principle of identity between thinking and being, Hegel held that, in philosophy, there is also an identity between the theory that concerns being, that is to say, ontology, and the theory that concerns the laws and the forms of thought, that is to say, logic. While, as in the identity of being and thought, thought is principal and being is secondary, Hegel then comes to consider that logic is the soul of ontology such that ontology has logic as a foundation.

Hegel held thought as first and being as second, and he made logic the foundation of ontology. This is manifestly the fundamental principle of Hegel's idealist philosophy. However, here the rational kernel of Hegelian philosophy resides in the fact that, at the interior of an idealist philosophy, he correctly guessed the unity of the laws of thought and the laws of objectivity, the coincidence of ontology and logic. As Lenin said: 'Hegel actually *proved* that logical forms and laws are not an empty shell, but the *reflection* of the objective world. More correctly, he did not prove, but *made a brilliant guess*'.[18]

More than this, the rational kernel of Hegelian philosophy also resides here in the fact that he underlined the 'active character' [*caractère agissant*] of thought. [NOTE J, see below p. 74] We know that human thought cannot only reflect the objective world but equally, by pushing forth from known objective laws, can act and have an influence on the objective world, thereby transforming what was only found in thought—like an ideal, project, program, etc.—into real being; the objective world is thus subordinated and belongs to it. The Hegelian point of view whereby things are the exteriorization of thought, where the exteriorized is negated and then returns to thought, develops this subjective activity of human consciousness in an idealist fashion.

Hegel's idea of the coincidence between the logical and the historical is the concrete manifestation, in his philosophy, of the principle of identity between of thought and being. Hegel held that, since there is an identity between thought and being, the process of the development of thought and knowledge, and the development of being advances side by side. The first is what we call the 'logical', the second is what we call 'historical'; the two coincides. Let us again take the examples in the *Logic* and in the conception of history in Hegel's philosophy: when we explained Hegel's idea in the above that knowledge is a process which goes from the abstract toward the concrete, from the simple towards the complex, we said that the development of the concepts of Hegel's *Logic* and the development of the history of philosophy follows this process that goes from the

18. Lenin, 'Science de la Logique de Hegel'. [Lenin, *Conspectus of Hegel's Science of Logic*, retrieved 1 December 2008, <http://marxists.org/archive/lenin/works/1914/cons-logic/ch03.htm>.]

abstract towards the concrete, from the simple to the complex. Why do the two courses of development coincide? It is certainly not by chance. This is precisely the manifestation of the principle of the coincidence between logic and history. What we understand here by logic designates the process of the development of the history of philosophy. It is precisely from the basis of this principle that Hegel considers the historical order of appearance of philosophical systems and the order of the deduction of logical concepts as the same. From the basis of this principle, Hegel had roughly established parallel and corresponding relations between the order of logical concepts in logic and the order of the appearance of the philosophical systems in the history of philosophy. Thus, in logic, there is a category, Being: it is the most original category, the most abstract and the most poor. Corresponding to this category, there is, in the history of philosophy, the philosophy of Parmenides, for whom the fundamental principle is the Absoluteness of Being. Hegel considered the place where logic begins as the commencement of the history of philosophy. That is why a true history of philosophy always begins, for Hegel, with the philosophy of Parmenides. In logic, there is the category of 'becoming', and there is, in the history of philosophy, a corresponding philosophy, the philosophy of Heraclitus: it considers 'becoming' as the fundamental character of things. Along with this, in the history of philosophy, that which corresponds to the logical category of 'being-in-itself' is the philosophy Democritus. What corresponds to the logical category of substance is the philosophy of Spinoza; and what corresponds to the ultimate category, the supreme but also the most concrete, Absolute Idea, is the philosophy of Hegel himself. However, Hegel held that a total coincidence between logic and history is impossible, and that is why this sort of parallel relation and the correspondences described in the above are not absolute. For, in effect, real history always includes contingencies, it may have deviations, but, from a logical point of view, these are contingent phenomena, these are phenomena of deviation [NOTE K, see below p. 75] to be put aside. Also, what is logical, or under the purview of logic, is the placing contingency outside of real history. In speaking of the parallelism and the coincidence between the development of logical concepts and the development of the history of philosophy, Hegel underlines that these relations of parallelism and coincidence are not to be referred to 'but at a level of a whole', or 'approximately'.

We have only taken in the above the example of the history of metaphysics for explaining the coincidence of logic and history. In fact, for

Hegel, it is not only the history of the development of metaphysics that coincides with the development of logical concepts, it is equally the case that the history of the development of everything real; the process of the development of everything real is also a process that goes from simple to complex, where the content unceasingly enriches itself. Hegel considered everything present as a result of something in the past; the ultimate result of historical development is like a great stream of water, the further it flows, the greater its volume, that is to say, the content becomes more and more enriched.

In summarizing his thought on the coincidence between logic and history, Hegel thought, in rearranging everything, that history is nothing but the result of the development of logical concepts: this is clearly idealism. But the strict ties between the logical and the historical constitute the rational part of his philosophy. From the point of view of scientific materialism, the course of thought that goes from the simple to the complex (logic) corresponds to a real historical process. Marx's *Capital* is the best example of a study of the principle of the coincidence of logic and history. Marx first studies commodity then money, and then capital. Here, commodity is the simplest category. Money is more complex than commodity. Capital is more complex than money. According to the process of knowledge, if we do not first understand the simple things, we cannot understand the complex things; this is why such a process of examination that goes from the examination of commodity to that of capital is not incidental or arbitrary, but determined by the logical order of thought, by the necessity of the process of knowledge. But, on the other hand, logic is the theoretical expression of real historical development, and the process of deduction of categories that goes from commodity to money and from money to capital is also determined by real historical development. These three things appear, in real historical development, according to an order that goes from simple to complex, from the inferior to the superior—from commodity to money, from money to capital: the appearance of money is later than commodity and capital later than money. After having explained all this, Marx indicated: 'To that extent the path of abstract thought, rising from the simple to the combined, would correspond to the real historical process'.[19]

19. [Marx, *Grundrisse*, p. 102.]

VI. The principle relative to the coincidence between logic and theory of knowledge

From this principle of the identity of thought and Being, Hegel held, on the one hand, that logic and ontology coincide, and on the other hand, that logic and the theory of knowledge also coincide. The theory of knowledge is the theory concerning the process of knowledge; the content of that knowledge is existent things (being). Logic is the theory concerning the forms of thought but Hegel held that the forms of thought studied by dialectical logic are not arcane and abstract formulas, cut off from the content of knowledge but are rather strictly tied to the content: to a precise content and form. The order of the forms of thought—concepts and categories—that Hegel's logic studies is then not at all arbitrary, but coincides with the process of the development of knowledge and, with that, the course of the deepening the incessant concretization of the content of knowledge. If Hegel's logic parts ways with the concept of Being, it is because the knowledge that we have of concrete things at the start is lacking and abstract. As such, when we have something like Being but cannot say anything about it, the content of our knowledge is thus the lacking and abstract; the logical category corresponding to this stage of knowledge is Being. The categories which follow Being all correspond, for Hegel, to the content of knowledge. And, in the process of knowledge, we first have direct sensible knowledge and only after this do we penetrate the essence of things. While in logic, the category of Being appears first and Essence follows afterwards, in process of knowledge, knowledge of quantity demands a deeper understanding than quality. While in logic the category of quality appears first followed quantity, in the process of knowledge, the knowledge of dialectical relations between such and such a thing is more profound than the simple understanding of a thing, here also we first have the category of a Thing and then that of Causality, etc. In brief, the development of knowledge follows a course that goes from the abstract towards the concrete, from the simple towards the complex. The deduction of logical categories follows the same course. The two coincide. Even if the order of conversion of Hegel's logical categories is something forced or rigid, its logic as a whole lays out, in an idealist fashion, a rational dialectical thought of the coincidence between logic and the theory of knowledge.

For better understanding the coincidence between logic and the theory of knowledge in Hegel, we will approach more particularly the problem of different types of judgement in the logic of Hegel: as we have said in the above, concrete truth is, for Hegel, the organic unity of many determinations. From this fundamental point of view, Hegel affirms that judgement is not an category exterior to or parallel with concrete truth but the development of it, the exposition and the explication of the particularities or determinations that comprises concrete truth. Let's take the judgement: 'gold is yellow'. 'Yellow' is an exposition of a particularity of this thing that is 'gold'. From this perspective of judgement, Hegel, for the first time in the history of philosophy, had, in sticking close to content of knowledge [NOTE L, see below p. 78], distinguished three great stages and four main types of judgement.

The three great stages are that of Being, Essence and the Concept, corresponding to the three major parts of the *Logic*. The judgement at the stage of Being is the 'essential judgement'; the judgement at the stage of Essence comprises 'reflective judgement' and 'necessary judgement'; and the judgement at the stage of the Concept is called the 'conceptual judgement'. These four types of judgement are not at the same level and do not have the same value; there is a hierarchy, a given order. Each judgment that follows occupies a more elevated place that its precedent. Let us take for example (1) 'roses are red', (2) 'roses are useful', (3) 'roses are plants', (4) 'This bouquet of roses is beautiful'. According to the content of knowledge, the sense of the predicates, the four types of judgement become increasingly elevated: the first ('the roses are red') is the most inferior such that the predicate of this type of judgement does not layout anything but the particular direct and sensible qualities of the subject (roses, concrete things). For determining if the subject does or does not have this quality, it is sufficient to use our immediate sensations. For example, if we want to determine if the rose has this quality of redness, it is sufficient simply to use our sight. Hegel called these judgements 'essential judgements'. This type of judgement shows that the content of knowledge has not yet attained the essence of the thing, it is not but direct and immediate; this type of judgement is but a stage of Being, and we cannot say that it is equivalent to that of Essence.

The second type of judgement, such as 'the roses are useful', are called 'reflective judgement'. The account of the predicate of this judgment does not only concern the particular direct and sensible qualities but the determinations relative to certain connections of the subject. In effect, saying that 'roses are useful' bears the trait of the relation between roses and other things; this type of judgement accounts for the particularities of roses from their relation with other things. Hegel held that this judgement touched on the essence of things, such that, for him, the category of a thing is the 'reflection on itself' in a relation. This judgement manifestly gives an account the content of the subject in a more concrete and profound way. This judgement is thus at a level above essential judgment.

Higher than the 'reflective judgement' is the 'necessary judgement', such as 'roses are plants'. The account of predicates of this type of judgement are the relations between the substance and the subject; like the 'reflective judgement', it belongs to the stage of Essence, but it comprises more necessity, it more profoundly and more concretely accounts for the content and the particularities of the subject. This type of judgement is thus superior.

However, the judgment that most profoundly and concretely accounts for the content and particularities of the subject is yet a fourth type of judgement, the 'conceptual judgement'. This judgment shows whether a concrete thing (the subject) corresponds with its nature, with its concept, and to what degree it corresponds. Thus the predicates 'beautiful', 'true', 'good' ... For example: 'this bouquet of roses is beautiful', 'this house is good'. These judgements always compare a concrete thing to its concept, they compare 'this bouquet of roses' to the concept of 'rose'; they compare 'this house' and the concept of 'house'. Everything that corresponds to its concept, to its nature, is then beautiful, good and true. Also, when we say: 'this bouquet of roses are beautiful', it means that this bouquet of flowers has grown in conformity with its nature, to the concept of rose. When we say: 'this house is good', this means that this house has been constructed in conformity with the concept of the house. Hegel held that, by forming such a judgement, it is necessary to have the most profound and concrete knowledge of concrete things.

Hegel's classification may certainly seem a little forced and obscure. When, in particular, he makes the apodictic judgment the unique and supreme judgment, this is where we find a manifestation of the idealist nature of his philosophy; however, as Engels said: 'the inner truth and necessity of this grouping will become clear...'[20]

20. [Friedrich Engels, *The Dialectic of Nature*, trans. Clemens Dutt, retrieved 1 December

His classification places the different forms of judgement at higher and lower levels according to the process of the deepening of knowledge and thus profoundly describes the process of knowledge that one finds with concrete truth which goes from the abstract and indigent towards the concrete and profound: when the content of our knowledge is only the immediate existence of the object, or nothing but the particular abstract and sensible qualities, when our knowledge is only superficial and abstract, the form of thought that we use, the form of judgement, is the most inferior judgement, the 'essential judgment' ; when the content of our knowledge of being ranges over the determination of the relations of the object, when it penetrates the 'essence' of the object, when our knowledge is more profound, the more concrete, the form of thought that we use is 'reflective judgment' or even 'necessary judgment'. What the 'conceptual judgment' expresses is that we have the most profound and concrete knowledge of the object. For each sort of content of knowledge, there is a type of form of knowledge; the content of knowledge incessantly deepens itself and concretizes itself and the same goes for the form of knowledge; the whole of the conceptual system of Hegel's logic concretely demonstrates the principle of unity of the logic and knowledge. Of course, this principle is demonstrated by Hegel under an idealist form.

We have outlined in the above some important dialectical ideas of Hegel's system; in fact, the rational thought of the Hegel's philosophical system is much richer than what we have developed here. Even in the 'philosophy of nature', the weakest link in Hegelian philosophy, there are quite a few rational ideas. The ideas we cited when we spoke earlier of the natural stage are clear proof of this. In *Ludwig Feuerbach and the End of Classical German Philosophy*, Engels said that it does not suffice to uselessly stop at the foot of the great edifice that is the idealist system of Hegelian philosophy, but rather, in penetrating it, we discover innumerable treasures.[21] This praise by Engels is not at all excessive.

Even though what Hegel says is certainly not the dialectic of the objective world, in the dialectic of Absolute Spirit or Absolute Idea, in the process of reciprocal relation, mutual conversion, and the self contradiction of purely logical concepts, in a word, in his idealist dialectic, he divined

---

2008, <http://www.marxists.org/archive/marx/works/1883/don/ch07c.htm>.]

21. [Friedrich Engels, *Ludwig Feuerbach and the End of Classical German Philosophy*, trans. Progress Publishers, Progress Publishers, retrieved 1 December 2008, <http://www.marxists.org/archive/marx/works/1886/ludwig-feuerbach/ch01.htm>.]

or, rather, he unconsciously reflected the dialectic of objective things themselves. For example, in Hegel's ideas with respect to movement and the incessant development of Absolute Spirit or the Absolute Idea, and the existence of internal relations in movement and development, we find that they unconsciously reflect the real situation of movement and incessant development of the real world where mutual and reciprocal relations condition all these phenomena. Equally, in Hegel's ideas on the self-movement of Spirit, of the Idea, where contradictions are the source of movement, and on idea of the reciprocal conversion of the two concepts 'quality' and 'quantity': these ideas also unconsciously reflected the real situation of internal contradictions and the transformations between quality and quantity in the real world. And even Hegel's ideas found in the process of the self-knowledge of Spirit, of Idea, a process that goes from the abstract to the concrete, from the simple to the complex, there again we find that they unconsciously reflect the process of deeper understanding and the incessant concretization of real human knowledge. And so forth.

In brief, in his idealist dialectic, in the dialectic of the concept, 'Hegel brilliantly divined the dialectics of things (phenomena, the world, nature)....'[22]

He had unconsciously reflected the dialectic of objective things themselves; therein resides the 'rational kernel' of Hegel's dialectic and it great historical merit.

Before the construction of Marxist philosophy, there were two methods that concerned the question of the development of the sciences: the first was the metaphysical method; the other was the Hegelian dialectic. However, the old method of metaphysics certainly could not have stimulated the development of the sciences, it was already destroyed in Kant's theoretical schema and above all by Hegel; only the Hegelian method posed the problem of universality and the eternity of the dialectic development; it tried to make the world a process of movement, of transformation and incessant development, and to discover internal relations within them; it had 'an enormous historical feeling as a foundation'. When it comes to the study of problems, it often takes the point of view of development and relation; Hegelian dialectics was thus, at the time, 'among the existing logical materials the only material that is at least usable'. These are precisely the rational elements that Marx and Engels

22. [Lenin, *Conspectus of Hegel's Science of Logic*, retrieved 1 December 2008, <http://www.marxists.org/archive/lenin/works/1914/cons-logic/ch03.htm>]

had assimilated from Hegelian dialectic when they had created dialectical materialism.

Hence, this is why the great Marxist-Leninist authors had highly appreciated the philosophy of Hegel.

However, the dialectic of Hegel, with respect to its essence, is fundamentally idealist [NOTE M, see below p. 80]. It is built from an anti-scientific basis; Hegel has only guessed the dialectic of objective things in his idealist dialectic and he did not have a scientific knowledge of the real objective process that appears dialectically. On the contrary, he had, under an idealist (mystical) form, fundamentally deformed this real objective process. This is why Hegelian dialectics 'in its existing form is unusable' and, in assimilating the rational part of Hegel's dialectical method, Marx and Engels thus thought that it was necessary first to make a radical critique of Hegel's method, and by penetrating and 'rejecting his idealist residue', the dialectic might appear under its original aspect.

Commentary to
The Rational Kernel of the Hegelian Dialectic

(a) On being, nothing, becoming

I. The idealism of the passage from being to nothing

The idealism at the start of the logic will come from the taking place of a commencement, or if one is to be more rigorous about it, rather than saying that the one (Being) transforms itself into the other (nothing), we should say that there is a problematic of commencement.

Caught in the commencement, the Hegelian dialectic does not develop itself through the form of the work of contradiction. It functions differently: we begin with a unique term, being, and soon there is the appearance of a form of repetition, of a logic of difference where the motor is not the process of the division of identity, nor a process of the fusion of contraries (being and nothing resolving each other in becoming). Rather it is a double inscription of identity under the form of two marks for which the referent is absolutely undifferentiated: being and nothing are two marks for the void. The commencement for Hegel will then be understood as the position of the same term twice. What finds itself thusly inscribed by Hegel is the weakest sort of difference, the difference of two identical marks (two marks for the void) and their marking out of two different places, two marks that do not differ except for their place.

This passage from one term to another, when they are identical, drives toward, in reality, a serial logic, taking the one then the other as minimal difference: a term dissipates into the other that is identical to it...

We can give an immediately formalizable mode for what we find going on here, a logical matrix that shows a process that re-seizes itself and thus integrates a certain idea of movement but does not move any further than iteration; this is movement in the sense of locomotion, the movement of the same, of the one, but not transformation. Thus:

- suppose that a marking occurs in a space of inscription: the commencement (for Hegel, the inscription of being);
- right away, another term is retroactively constituted: the blank on which this mark has just been inscribed. Once a mark is inscribed, it establishes that on which it marks. What is then constituted, in turn, is a difference between the term and what is not the inscription (the ground). We have a mark, but in a certain sense, we have two givens: the mark and its ground.

The result is that we will need to inscribe this difference of itself to itself, at least if one does not want to leave a remainder. To avoid any sort of discordance between the term and the process of inscription, it is thus necessary to mark the base.

We will then inscribe a second mark (the nothing, for Hegel). But these two marks are the same: we have marked a difference, but that with which we have marked this difference is a repetition. We thus have a first mark (being) and a second (nothing) which takes the ground into account. However, once again there is something that is not marked, the difference of these two marks, that which would make their identity a difference of itself to itself.

It is this difference that it is now necessary to mark, the difference of the first two. Becoming, for Hegel, will then be interpreted as the marking of this difference between being and nothing. Yet at the same time, it will be nothing without the concrete existence of their identity.

We move forward in this way through a process of the engendering of an infinite iteration following what was given in germination by the marking of being and nothing. We are certainly here at a rational kernel but it concerns analytic logic and numerical thought, and not the dialectic:

1. marking
2. retroactive causality that causes the mark never to be equal to itself,
3. re-marking or repetition that, in turn, causes a term to emerge that is not marked, or the difference of the two first marks,
4. I inscribe this difference, etc.

The motor of this process is the set of voids retroactively constituted by the marks (there is always somewhere a void place, an unmarked) and not the scission of identity.

II. Iteration, then, and not dialectics

However, to stick to the initial project, it is necessary now to ask ourselves whether Hegel has nonetheless reflected the dialectic of things and objective phenomena in this passage.

Since the idealism of the being-nothing passage has been previously assimilated under repetition and not dialectic (scission of identity), asking what the rational aspects are, consists above all to see whether the work of contradiction exists despite the intertwined presence of its immediate contrary, iteration.

In fact, iteration is not the only motor here and its double status of becoming is the proof of this:

- as an iterative term, it comes in at the third position to mark the identity of being and nothing.
- Yet, contradictorily, in this same chapter, Hegel will see to restoring an absolute difference between being and nothing: 'But it is equally true that they are not undistinguished from each other, that, on the contrary, they are not the same, that they are absolutely distinct, and yet that they are unseparated and inseparable....'[1]

Hence we find Being and nothing understood as contraries after having been confounded iteratively by a becoming that marks only their particular difference in place and that only succeeds at inscribing one identity to another. What is being posed hence, is no longer becoming-identity, the third term of iteration, but a becoming-unity of contraries.

And from this perspective, we might continue in affirming that, at its starting place, Hegel makes place for contradiction.

But it is necessary to see how this is the case, that is to say, at the interior of what project, and due to what insurmountable contradictions.

Hence something of the Hegelian enterprises fails here. It is nothing less that the attempt to generate the concept (in this case, a concept that integrates the idea of contradiction, becoming) in continuity with the one (pure being...), the immediate, and the *surrender* [*l'abandon*] to the life of the object.[2] In the one case becoming inscribes the identity of two terms, and on the other, their absolute difference. From the same fact, we sufficiently see that this second becoming cannot align itself with the

1. [Hegel, *Science of Logic*, p. 83.]

2. [Hegel, *Phenomenology of Spirit*, trans. by A.V. Miller, Oxford, Oxford University Press, 1977, p. 32.]

iterative order where it was presumed to proceed. The latter, in effect, is defined only in never being able to support the inscription of a strong difference. Radically heterogeneous, becoming-contradiction cannot then share a place except by a forcing [*forçage*]. Such is the very impression left by this 'passage'.

Wanting at any price to peg in the two (becoming-contradiction) to the one (pure being), yet under the law and the premise of the one (iteration), Hegel saw the constraint of going about this with unsanctioned force [*coup de force*]: he reintroduced, totally exterior to iteration, what cannot by itself be inscribed: the two.

This insurmountable contradiction, where we find the opposite (discontinuity) of what he wanted to demonstrate (continuity), will also take the form of an impossible passage from the successive (being-nothing) to the simultaneous (being and nothing). To becoming, Hegel assigns the role of being the pivot of this toggling, but the whole contradiction of the project will be re-concentrated upon it. In a connected association, he could not but juxtapose it [becoming] as being one (of two fusioned into one) and one (which divides into two), or really two, in its proper peculiarity. We can see this in the beginning of the chapter:

> 'c. becoming (author's note: as iterative term)
> 1. Unity of being and nothing (author's note: internal contradiction)'[3]

Thus presupposed in its continuity even in an unsuccessful way, this eruption of heterogeneity goes on, like a clinamen, to enfold the rest of the text which was otherwise condemned to the sterile operation of a coordinated iteration.

And, whether as 'demonstrated', 'derived', or at least presupposed, insofar as there is a continuity between the iterative and the contradictory, a successful genesis from the contradictory encounter of being/nothing solely from their iterative succession, Hegel could already, a second time (2. Moments of becoming)[4], make a return to the commencement, to clarify, to enrich this contradictory encounter, to re-inscribe it in a double commencement:

> Becoming is in this way in a double determination. In one of them, nothing is immediate, that is, the determination starts from nothing which relates itself to being, or in other words, changes into it; in the other, being is immediate, that is, the

3. [Hegel, *Science of Logic*, p. 82.]
4. [Hegel, *Science of Logic*, p. 105.]

> determination starts from being which changes into nothing: the former is coming-to-be and the latter ceasing-to-be.[5]

This forced insertion of becoming-contradiction has thus the immediate effect of repeating the first iteration: in place of one commencement, there will be two.

What is more interesting is the third time (3. sublation of becoming),[6] it can, just as in the case of Becoming, provide some matter for division. Here, it is 'sublations' in plural that should be understood.

Having thus preserved himself with the rights of iteration (double ***Commencement***) and that of contradiction (***double*** commencement), Hegel does nothing more than to reiterate the contradiction proper to becoming. It is sublation itself that comes to be envisaged in two ways:

- following the law of repetition which takes into account the notions of 'equilibrium', 'stable unity'... proper to an iterative thread in which identity is primary: 'The resultant equilibrium of coming-to-be and ceasing-to-be is in the first place becoming itself. But this equality settles into a stable unity. Being and nothing are in this unity only as vanishing moments; yet becoming as such is only through their distinguishedness. Their vanishing, therefore, is the vanishing of becoming or the vanishing of the vanishing itself. Becoming is an unstable unrest which settles into a stable result'.[7]
- or, sublation-contradiction directly articulated as the contradictory itself of becoming: 'This could also be expressed thus: becoming is the vanishing of being in nothing and of nothing in being and the vanishing of being and nothing generally; but at the same time it rests on the distinction between them. It is therefore inherently self-contradictory, because the determinations it unites within itself are opposed to each other; but such a union destroys itself'.[8]

That Hegel does not make a clear break and does not arrive at conceiving the incompatibility of the two types of sublation again demonstrates his repeated intention to reconcile the two: the articulation of the one and the two under the law of the one. This is the content of what he names *aufhebung* (overcoming—raising up) [*dépassement-relève*], a term that he

5. [Hegel, *Science of Logic*, p. 105-6.]

6. [Hegel, *Science of Logic*, p. 106.]

7. [Hegel, *Science of Logic*, p. 106.]

8. [Hegel, *Science of Logic*, p. 106.]

will follow immediately with the comment that it is 'a fundamental determination which repeatedly occurs throughout...'[9]

In the guise of a conclusion and as a last take on this division of the text, we will note that this internal contradiction at start of the logic (iteration/contradiction) will be found accounted elsewhere in the short text that precedes the first chapter: 'With what must the science begin?'[10]

To this question Hegel formulates two responses, direct and/or indirect commencement, subjective and/or objective commencement... which in the sum that covers the difference.

- between an iterative commencement from pure being: the commencement 'must be purely and simply *an* immediacy, or rather merely *immediacy* itself. Just as it cannot possess any determination relative to anything else, so too it cannot contain within itself any determination, any content; for any such would be a distinguishing and an inter-relationship of distinct moments, and consequently a mediation. The beginning therefore is pure being'.[11]
- and a commencement-contradiction privileging becoming: 'The analysis of the beginning would thus yield the notion of the unity of being and nothing—or, in a more reflected form, the unity of differentiatedness and non-diffrentiatedness, or the identity of identity and non-identity'.[12]

But even if well situated, this difference between the one and the other commencement, the one and the two... ends up being thought under a fundamental identity. As such, on the question of what comes first, Hegel will be split on whether to place the importance on pure being (subjective, immediate) or becoming (objective, mediate) as the point of departure such that 'the whole of the science be within itself a circle in which the first is also the last and the last is also the first...'.[13] As such, 'The progress does not consist merely in the derivation of an other, or in the effected transition into a genuine other...'.[14] Thus, if there only apparently is a one and a two, there is really only one, and if there is a two, it finds all its reason in the one....

9. [Hegel, *Science of Logic*, p. 107.]
10. [Hegel, *Science of Logic*, p. 67.]
11. [Hegel, *Science of Logic*, p. 70.]
12. [Hegel, *Science of Logic*, p. 74.]
13. [Hegel, *Science of Logic*, p. 71.]
14. [Hegel, *Science of Logic*, p. 71.]

Affirmations that prescribe and announce the idealism and the articulation at the start of the logic.

(b) On the interior and the exterior. Hegelian topology

The Hegelian theory of the rapport between essence/phenomenon provides a radical critique of the concept of the metaphysics of representation, where the object is in some matter given twice: in its true interiority and in its exteriority for us.

Hegel anticipates all thought that ruptures with immediate spatial schemas; founded on the opposition of inside and outside (the hidden inside being the truth of the merely apparent outside). To apprehend being as contradictory self-development, affirmative scission, is to pose that the exterior as being the same as the interior. Hegel sustains, against Kant, *a new topology of knowledge*.

The historical destiny of this topology is its inevitable division. We can in effect conceive it in a purely structural fashion: exterior and interior are to be discernable *at each point*, but indiscernible in the supposedly given all. We will say that there is a local subject of interior/exterior separation; however this demands an unconditional global unity of a law. This unity does not have any other evidence than its punctual effect, which is separation. The truth of the one is only insofar as it cannot be said *in whole* since the whole exists at each point as the act of a partition, of a two.

This path is followed by Lacan (but already by Mallarmé) in the usage that he makes of non-orientable surfaces like the mobius strip. In its global torsion, the ribbon does not admit to the distinction between interior and exterior. At each point, there is an 'inverse', thus an outside. As such, the all rematerializes as the scission interior/exterior, we need to cut the ribbon. We know that for Lacan this cut [*coupure*] is what precedes the subject: the subject is the act situated between the one of the all and its effect of the orientation of inside/outside. 'A' subject is the undoing of torsion.

But we can, and in fact we should conceive of the divided correlation of exterior/interior rather as a process that simultaneously places the real at its place and in excess over this place, at the interior and the exterior, residing in its deployment as qualitative force.

In this way, for example, the working class is at the same time an internal part of capitalist society (as exploited productive force) and a heterogeneous force to this society, essentially transmitting nothing but its destruction (insofar as being the revolutionary political class). From the point of view of the divided unity of the class, neither strict inclusion nor absolute exclusion is tenable. In reality the very existence of the proletariat impedes the thought of the capitalist 'system' as a pertinent totality furnished with an inside and outside. This is the root of the failure of all structuralist Marxisms, as with all the currents of 'leftism', that pretends to organize thought and action from an absolute comprehension of oppressive society as a system and hence advances the directive of dissidence, or 'exteriority'. The lack of an exterior does not signify an unsurpassable constraint at the interior (recuperation) any more than there is an interior.

On the common terrain (Hegelian) of dialectical topology which destroys the representative opposition of the interior/exterior, we need to oppose Lacan's subject-cut [*sujet-coupure*], for which lack is a fixed cause, with the subject-scission of dialectical materialism, for which the disorganization of force and place is a mobile cause.

(c) One divides into two

The expression has many meanings and might appear circular: Zhang says that this is because difference has, within itself, an identity that becomes difference. Is this an infinite evolution of these internal 'seeds'? In this case, do the new arrive since everything is entirely continuous with its antecedent dialectic?

Truth is what has *no identity other than from a difference*; hence the being of all things is the process of its division into two. For as much as we apprehend the qualitative identity of a force, it remains with respect to:

1. the place that it exceeds[15]
2. the structural system (system of distribution) that it destroys

Thus the actual revolutionary identity of the French proletariat is given in the excess of its place in union workerism [*l'ouvrierisme syndicalisant*] which has confined it in a long tradition and which constitutes itself as a political class driving for the destruction of the existing social system (French imperialism). However embryonic it might be, this identity (in terms of political practice and Maoist organization) always exists as a differential destroyer of an other. This is what it means for an identity to change itself in difference.

15. [reference originally cited in text] See Note g [see below p. 66].

(d) On the sense of the word 'critique'

In Chinese, there are two words that are generally translated for the sole word 'critique' [*critique*]. In fact, the first (*pi ping*),[16] to critique-comment, brings out the register of contradiction at the heart of the people. The second (*pi pan*),[17] to critique-judge, refers to more fundamental divergences and often indicates the register of antagonistic contradictions. It is this latter term that is employed in the Chinese text.

16. [批評]

17. [批判]

(e) On the category of negation

Formal logic is in reality an artificial construct [*dispositif artificiel*] (mathematics) that organizes formulae (the writing of formulae). Like all mechanic assemblages, this tool is itself without force: it does not 'work' over anything, and thus does not deliver any sort of truth. It is clear that in working through such a tool, we cannot, without destroying it (rendering it inconsistent), make it 'say', at the same time, a proposition and its negation. But the negation of a statement (of a formula) has absolutely nothing to do with the dialectic, which poses the being of things as the process of its scission. We could not say that the Hegelian tradition makes things any easier with its systematic usage of the word 'negation'. For what it's worth, the designation of this term in the phenomenon of language, a phenomenon from which we can extract a logical machine, does not designate anything in the real world. What exists can well be destructed, broken apart, but not rejected, and it is on account of a linguistic idealism that it is becomes necessary to carry on with the ontological usage of the category of negation.

Given its difficulties, especially concerning the dialectic of nature, it would make things less difficult if we were to radically eliminate the untenable idea of an objective negation. What would remain would be to hold on to the theme of the unity of contraries, but although 'contrariety' is presented as a single term, it produces, in fact, the disorganization of the other (its disappearing as a process of unification), and hence turns into other than what it was—as a term of another process. Division, destruction and alterity are here pertinent concepts, ones that 'negation' fusion together and renders in-operational.

It is clear from this that the intra-logical principle of non-contradiction is not an obstacle to dialectical thought, but is rather an absolutely particular region of human activity. In fact, it is only from historical materialism and dialectics that we can clear up the origin and the history of formal logic, as the artefact and rule of writing, in its specific connection to the history of mathematics.

(f) On the laws of dialectic

At the point that we are at, the enumeration of the characteristics of the 'rational kernel' follows quite closely to the indications that Engels makes in *The Dialectic of Nature* or *Anti-Düring*. We thus have three 'laws':

- the interdependence of the general movement of things
- contradiction
- change from quantitative to qualitative

A classical but narrow point of view, here comprising Lenin and Mao Zedong's reflections, took the third law (quantity/quality) as a particular case of the second because it designated the conversion of quantitative to qualitative as the realization of the unity of its contraries as quantity and quality.

The three 'laws' are equally erroneous .for not orienting the 'rational kernel' around its central point—the law of the unity of contraries - thus opening the path to its replacement by another central point: the principle of interdependence, or in fact, an even more vague principle of 'concrete totality'.[18]

These questions are essential because they focus reflection on the struggle between the two paths of the question of socialist transition. Should one consider socialist society principally as a totality in becoming, where the guarantee is the fixed point of state of the dictatorship of the proletariat? Or, on the contrary, should it be considered principally as a stage—completely new—of the bourgeois/proletarian contradiction? Is the dictatorship of the proletariat a *statist* concept of the hegemonized interdependence of phenomena or a political concept relative to the continuation of class struggle? Is the statist practice of the organization of everyone the condensation of the socialist experience, or is it the cultural revolutions that constitute the supreme political forms of class struggle, aiming at the dissolution of the state?

18. [reference originally cited in text] On this see Badiou, *Théorie de la contradiction*, ch. 2. [Alain Badiou, *Théorie de la contradiction,* Paris, Francois Maspero, 1975.]

Maoism cuts through this point: It is very much proletarian and revolutionary politics that remains the key to phenomena along the entire socialist transition. The state should be evaluated from the class struggle of the proletariat and not the reverse. In particular, under socialism, in the dialectic of state/revolution, it is the perspective class—and hence revolution—that is, with respect to the historical tasks of the proletariat, the principal aspect of contradiction. This is the perspective from which the philosophical thesis of the strategic premise of the law of division (the political struggle of class) takes primacy over the law of totality (of statist stability).

(g) Quantity and Quality: place, excess, destruction

In fact, the question has a double aspect.

All phenomena are simultaneously a qualitative interiority and an ascending or descending quantity. But the vague association of quantity with number or measure is an obstacle to the dialectical grasping of the quantity/quality relation.

We should call 'quantity' the form of variability (of movement) in phenomena such that, in its effects, does not modify the contradictory whole in which the phenomenon is inscribed insofar as it concerns its structural characteristics. Quantitative variation essentially leaves a thing *in its place*, since the structural character of contradiction resolves itself in a distribution of terms.

For example, the numerical augmentation of the working class or the rising number of Maoist militants are not facts that designate, *by themselves*, a structural transformation of the bourgeois/proletariat contradiction or the political relation between the working class avant-garde and modern revisionism even if it creates, with regard to this transformation, systems of new and essential constraints. We say that quantity is where the variability of the considered term remains subservient to a system of places.

Quality is in turn always differential: it does not exist in the heart of quantitative variation except as that which is in excess over the place of variation. The excess that is in contradiction with quantity in the exact measure is where its proper effect is the destruction of place.

It is thus why the political emergence of the working class or the practice of Maoist politics are, by themselves, rebellions against any prolonged assignations of a fixed system of the bourgeois/proletariat contradiction, or the Maoist/modern revisionist contradiction.

The relation of being to quality and quantity is thus not so much the question of 'proximity' but rather that of the *type of variability*. Quantity designates variation in place (conservative and extensive); quality is forced variation (destructive). The one designates the *integral* process of the given term (considered as included in an All); the other is its differential process (considered as heteronomous to the All).

Every entity is the contradictory movement of these two variations. To say that quantitative accumulation resolves itself in a qualitative jump means that the differential process finishes in 'self-integrating', that is to say, by no longer being qualitatively assignable in the space of the places that it occupied. It thus brings about, in this destroyed space, another structural figure of the distribution of places (and quantitative variations)

It is not quite exact to say that the quantitative summation produces the qualitative jump along a linear causality. In truth, the differential gap, at a certain stage of quantitative variation, *no longer has the place for being out of place* [*hors place*]. As such, a Maoist party that is quantitatively very powerful *can no longer* remain in simple excess with respect to the place ceded by the bourgeoisie to the revolutionary politics of the people. It is then necessary either to take power, or be brutally reduced. The second hypothesis is always present, and this is why there will never be a mechanical victory. This is precisely because the quantity/quality dialectic exists at every stage of the development of phenomenon and does not arise through accumulation.

This holds also because quantitative variation does not by itself produce a new place, but only poses a limitation of the possibility of a differential affirmation of the system of existing places.

(h) History of Philosophy, real history, Glucksmann, Heidegger

'[T]he study of the history of Philosophy is an introduction to Philosophy itself'.[19] This is true if by the history of philosophy we understand philosophy in its relation to the real world and not as the self-arising of the concept, philosophical eschatology. Here as elsewhere, there are then two possible accounts of Hegel.

1. The first, starting from a philosophy that has 'as foundation an enormous historical sentiment' (Marx) works to take Hegel's materialist idea at its terms, understanding philosophers as a 'mirror of the whole history'.[20]

2. The other idea of Hegel holds, above all, that the history of self-realization of the concept, of the idea ... briefly put, that ideas drive the world such that outside, the real material world, makes it possible to establish a connection between the different philosophical systems, thus to think of them in their history in an autonomous way. Marx analysed this conception in the following way:

> The whole trick of proving the hegemony of the spirit in history (hierarchy, Stirner calls it) is thus confined to the following three efforts.
>
> 1) One must separate the ideas of those ruling for empirical reasons, under empirical conditions and as empirical individuals, from these actual rulers, and thus recognise the rule of ideas or illusions in history.
>
> 2) One must bring an order into this rule of ideas, prove

19. [Hegel, *Lectures on the History of Philosophy*, retrieved December 1 2008, <http://marxists.org/reference/archive/hegel/works/hp/hpintro.htm>.]

20. [Hegel, *Lectures on the History of Philosophy*, retrieved December 1 2008, <http://marxists.org/reference/archive/hegel/works/hp/hpintro.htm>.]

> a mystical connection among the successive ruling ideas, which is managed by understanding them as 'acts of self-determination on the part of the concept' (this is possible because by virtue of their empirical basis these ideas are really connected with one another and because, conceived as mere ideas, they become self-distinctions, distinctions made by thought).
>
> 3) To remove the mystical appearance of this 'self-determining concept' it is changed into a person—'Self-Consciousness'—or, to appear thoroughly materialistic, into a series of persons, who represent the 'concept' in history, into the 'thinkers', the 'philosophers', the ideologists, who again are understood as the manufacturers of history, as the 'council of guardians', as the rulers. Thus the whole body of materialistic elements has been removed from history and now full rein can be given to the speculative steed.[21]

Here we have, in a certain way, the whole program of the 'new' philosophy *['nouvelle' philosophie]*: the history of philosophy as self-realization, determination of concepts of the state and the gulag: the master thinkers as the makers of history.

To oppose them with an elementary materialism would not but be an oblique force and would not then constitute any kind of response in the face of those which depict themselves as a new idealism such as the 'new' philosophers do. It doesn't hurt to remind oneself of this.

Not in the least, this permits us to seize this wave in its elementary idealist dimension.

What Glucksmann considers as the relation of philosophy to history is already a pure and simple inversion of the materialist thesis of the primacy of reality over thought.

Here, thought is not conceived as that which first and principally reflects reality. Real history is not what is reflected in a text nor is it, at its limits, a relation to text (and in that sense, otherwise ignored by Glucksmann, there would have been many things to say about the relation between the text and its reader presupposed in its Hegelian introductions and prefaces). Between text and reality, it is the text that is principal for Glucksmann, in the sense where for example:

21. [reference originally cited in text] *L'idéologie allemande*, Editions sociales, p. 78. [Karl Marx, 'The German Ideology', in *The Marx Engels Reader*, 2nd ed., Robert C. Tucker (ed.), trans. W. Lough, New York and London, W.W. Norton and Co., p. 175.]

> The 'Germany' where Fascisms are born is not a territory or a population but a text and an attitude to texts which became established long before Hitler.[22]

In this history of fascisms and gulags, there is an adequation of text and territory, of thought and reality. But, for Glucksmann, the force of this adequation is to be found in the active side of text and thought: history does nothing but to realize the text of the master thinkers.

> Equivalence of a text with a territory—true, for the last five hundred years, and with some exceptions. But it is in the armed institution of the text that we have to see the active side of this equivalence: the text lays down the law for the territory.[23]

There would then be no history other than the strategy of text:

> Texts do not simply serve the exercise of power, they are that very exercise, they subject people. Even more than the chains of slavery, they are part of that slavery. Policemen inside the heads of those who subjected them, the great texts of power in Europe are not in the service of the strategies of domination, they are these strategies themselves.[24]

The history of the real folded in the law of the master thinkers' texts, history enters 'a strange Germany whose text did not correspond to its territory, a Germany that would belong to yesterday and tomorrow but never today'.[25]

Curiously, this is to completely reject Hegel ('Successive generations have striven to isolate out from Hegel's work a body of left-wing thought, a revolutionary method which they contrast with the right-wing system of the alleged 'official philosopher' of the Prussian state. They are victims of optical illusions: whether his left or his right profile be looked at, one and the same Hegel appears to our view'[26]), and not to divide it. With

22. [reference originally cited in text] André Glucksmann, *Les maîtres penseurs*, [Paris, Grasset, 1977,] p. 40. [André Glucksmann, *The Master Thinkers*, trans. Brian Pearce, New York, Harper and Row, 1980, p. 37.]

23. [reference originally cited in text] Glucksmann, *Les maîtres penseurs*, p. 42. [Glucksmann, *The Master Thinkers*, p. 38.]

24. [reference originally cited in text] Glucksmann, *Les maîtres penseurs*, p. 51. [Glucksmann, *The Master Thinkers*, p. 47.]

25. [reference originally cited in text] Glucksmann, *Les maîtres penseurs*, p. 43. [Glucksmann, *The Master Thinkers*, p. 39.]

26. [reference originally cited in text] Glucksmann, *Les maîtres penseurs*, p. 174. [Glucksmann, *The Master Thinkers*, p. 165.]

this we rapidly repeat idealism, in Glucksmann as in Hegel, there would be no history other than the realization of Spirit and further only exclusively 'in the form that is its complete realization: the State'.

No doubt, what remains is the question of the *plebs* [*plèbe*], the free-pass of this idealism.[27] However, putting aside the fact that this conception of the *pleb* has the effect of re-inscribing the entire book into contradiction, that insofar as we have liquefied them, we can take them into account, (if indeed, 'The master thinkers thus overtake each other [...] in the *plebs*',[28] if each one of them 'cries victory when he discovers those whom his predecessor has left on the shelf [...]', what is left then for Glucksmann?)[29] What else can we say to this *pleb* if not to convince her, in silence, of the Heideggerian task? Closer to the *pleb*, it is on this question that Greek philosophy is silent. But worse, as with technology in Heidegger, it is with the gulags in Glucksmann that we need to polish the missed encounters of the realization of history to recover the lost sense of the *pleb*.

Such are the sources of Glucksmann's short reverences for Heideggerian idealism.

27. [One of Glucksmann's central critiques of political thought in *Les maîtres penseurs* turns around the term '*plèbe*' which he uses to criticize the German tradition (Fichte, Hegel) concerning the *Pöbel*, the rabble or what is later to be thought of, in the Marxist tradition, as *lumpenproletariat*. The use of *pleb* in the translation follows Brian Pearce's translation of *The Master Thinkers* which I have been using. See Glucksmann, *The Master Thinkers*, p. 167-169.]

28. [reference originally cited in text] Glucksmann, *Les maîtres penseurs*, 175. [Glucksmann, *The Master Thinkers*, p. 164.]

29. [reference originally cited in text] Glucksmann, *Les maîtres penseurs*, p. 174. [Glucksmann, *The Master Thinkers*, p. 163.]

(i) Class struggle on thought and being

The identity of thought and being had been the theme of a particularly bitter philosophical struggle between 1958 and 1963 in China, one that the author, Zhang Shiying, had personally participated. It was him, among others, who brought the position of Marxist philosophy to this question: Does the affirmation and the negation of the identity between thought and being trace a line of demarcation between those who held that thought is in a state of understanding the real world and those who pose the existence of an unbridgeable barrier between the two?;[30] Does the affirmation or the negation of the relations between thought and being as a dialectical identity allow us to distinguish dialectical materialism and its mechanistic and revisionist deviation which fetishises 'objective conditions'? Mao Zedong's text, 'Where do correct ideas come from' is in part a philosophical intervention tied directly to this debate and to the political conjuncture weaved by the Great Leap Forward: against the philosopher Yang Hsien-Tchen[31] who wanted to hold to a strict 'materialist' position on the reflection of being through thought while, at the same time, saw the Great Leap Forward as 'voluntarist' and a 'petit bourgeois fever'. Mao affirmed in 1963: '[the] process leading from matter to consciousness and then back to matter'.[32] When Yang Hsien-tchen speaks of the Great Leap Forward and the movement of the people's communes as a 'waste' and attributed it to the 'identity between thought and being' and to an 'exaggeration of the subjective activity of man', he took himself to be mobilizing the masses.

---

30. [reference originally cited in text] cf. Engels, *Feuerbach et la Fin de la philosophie allemande*, 27-28. [Friedrich Engels, *Ludwig Feuerbach and the End of Classical German Philosophy*, trans. Progress Publishers, Progress Publishers, retrieved 1 December 2008, <http://www.marxists.org/archive/marx/works/1886/ludwig-feuerbach/ch01.htm>.]

31. [reference originally cited in text] cf. Badiou, *Théorie de la contradiction*, 63-66.

32. [Mao Zedong, 'Where do Correct Ideas come From?', in *Selected Works of Mao Tse-Tung*, vol. 9, Secunderabad, Kranti Publications, retrieved 1 December 2008, <http://marxists.org/reference/archive/mao/selected-works/volume-9/mswv9_01.htm>.]

It is interesting to note that the 2nd plenum of the IXth congress of the Chinese Communist Party, held at Lushan in August of 1970, was the theatre of a very lively struggle between the proletarian central committee and the partisans of the 'theory of the genius' [*théorie du génie*] grouped around Lin Biao. It took effect as a philosophical offensive that opened the critique of Lin Biao a year before his death: we are hence following a re-examination of the philosophical struggle over the identity of thought and being in China. It is, in effect, a metaphysical cut between thought and reality at work in the conceptions defended by Lin Biao, an 'innate' knowledge separated from the transformations of reality presenting the historical revolutionary leaders like 'geniuses' above history and the masses, even reversing the relation of the transformation of the subjective world to the objective world.

(J) On the term 'active character' [caractère agissant]

The term 'active character' has been used instead of 'activity' [*activité*], insofar as it better renders the idea of action as returning from the subjective to the objective. It refers to the philosophical concept of 'conscious activity' or 'subjective activity' developed by Mao Zedong in his military writing 'On Protracted war'.[33]

33. [reference originally cited in text] cf. *Oeuvres choisies* of Mao Zedong, vol. 2, p. 161-162, the chapter titled 'Man's Dynamic Role in War'. [Mao Zedong, On Protracted War, in *Selected Works of Mao Tse-Tung*, vol. 2, 1967, Beijing, Foreign Languages Press, retrieved 1 December 2008, <http://marxists.org/reference/archive/mao/selected-works/volume-2/mswv2_09.htm>.]

(k) The philosophical concept of deviation

Hegel's idealism also manifests itself in the absence of any positive theory of deviation. In an idealist conception of the dialectic, deviations do not and cannot exist. Why?

Deviations, setbacks ... are in fact not thinkable except in dialectic correlation with determination and the limit of a movement.

From this point of view, there are really two types of deviations (we currently designate them as: opportunism of the right and opportunism of the left). They do not emergence at the same time in the course of movement (one at the beginning and the other at the end).

To think of them as deviations presupposes seeing them as forces of repetition internal to contradiction, each one tends to re-invoke one of the terms of the initial contradiction:

- The former only repeats the dominant term
- and the second, in arguing for a state of original purity preceding all determination, will assign itself to the rediscovery of the other. It will always evoke this purity of origin for taking force historically.

We see then that the deviations are not referable except in their correspondence with the initial contradiction: In attesting to the very contradiction of development, it demonstrates that everything that occurs is deployed in the field of an initial contradiction.

However, what Hegel could not do was to think them in these terms, for he presupposed a single term rather than a contradiction.

On this basis, deviations do not have any necessity and 'all true thinking is a thinking of necessity'.[34] Its development does not integrate a

34. [Hegel, *Logic*, § 119 A2.]

struggle against deviations. 'What is actual is rational'[35] because it is necessary. Due to their contingency, deviations are then not real. To Hegel, reality is conceived under the mode of orthodoxy: it passes entirely through the other path.

On the contrary, Dialectical Materialism presents deviation as ineluctable, the existence of the false and the past at every stage of the process like a necessary law. There is no succession of the new from the past without a continual struggle between the two. The deviations are necessary and the struggle against deviations is an animating element of the development of the whole.

We will note that, despite all this, the absence of a positive theory of deviations does not constitute the whole of the Hegelian position.

It is on this question, along with many others, that we are confronted with the effects of the classical balancing act of the Hegelian system.

As we have seen, that there would be a single term rather than contradiction land us with ignoring the problem of deviations.

However, to take a true thought of contingency into account, one that integrates itself into the history of the concept[36], does not then reverse everything upon itself. For contingency implies necessity: 'the apparently contingent is necessary'.[37]

And at the same stroke, it would be real, etc.

What manifests itself here then is a typical contradiction in the Hegelian oeuvre, between the local and the whole, the explicit (what he says here about contingency) and the implicit (the general place of the struggle against deviations in the movement of the new), between theory and practice.

Another way of encircling this contradiction: insofar as the struggle against deviations is not conceived as a function of movement, it will then have the paradoxical effect of having to count on it and it alone for the genesis of the new. It is hence in this way that we should understand the connection between being→nothing→becoming. Here, Hegel finds himself cornered by his obstinacy for a single term. As such, to take an initial contradiction of pure white/being with the first mark, the nothing should in reality already be comprised as a previous step (re-invocation

35. [Hegel, *Elements of the Philosophy of Right*, ed. Allen W. Wood, trans. H.B. Nisbet, Cambridge, Cambridge University Press, 1991, p. 20.]

36. [originally cited in text] cf. Logic of essence, ch. 21, 'reality' [*La réalité, Wirklichkeit*]. [note that German *Wirklichkeit* in this usage is now translated as 'Actuality'. See Hegel, *Logic*, § 112-159 (The doctrine of essence) and § 142 (Actuality) .]

37. [Hegel, *Logic*, § 136 A2.]

of the initial dominant white). The return to being, in the chapter on the nothing, will hence be the recalling of the initial pure being. This is how, without presupposing anything but the past, Hegel will hold to inscribing the new to becoming. But we know that this strategy fails and there is a cut.

(I) 'In sticking close to the content' [En collant de près au contenu]

A well known aspect of the Hegelian system is found in one of the most celebrated formulations here in the preface of the *Phenomenology*:

> Scientific cognition, on the contrary, demands surrender to the life of the object, or, what amounts to the same thing, confronting and expressing its inner necessity.[38]

Through this, we find two ideas introduced:

1. Scientific knowledge should express the internal contradictions of things which they necessarily move, change and evolve.
2. To succeed in expressing these contradictions, for reaching this knowledge, it is necessary, Hegel tells us, to surrender oneself to the life of the object, it is necessary to go to the things...

- On the first aspect, the materialist dialectician plainly recognizes the premise of internal cause: 'The fundamental cause of the development of a thing is not external but internal; it lies in the contradictoriness within the thing'.[39] Here then is, on the question of internal causes as the principle of the development of things themselves, a connection between Hegel→Mao.
- On the second point, we have a problem. Otherwise put, one needs to divide the Hegelian proposal:

a) No one doubts that Hegel's phrase drives toward something of the sort: it is necessary for knowledge to pass through things themselves: correct ideas arise from practice... yes, but a practice drawn from which moment?

b) The whole question rests, certainly in Hegel, not with revolt but

38. [Hegel, *Phenomenology of Spirit*, p. 32.]

39. [Mao, On Contradiction, in *Selected Works of Mao Tse-Tung*, vol. 1, 1967, Beijing, Foreign Languages Press, retrieved 1 December 2008, <http://marxists.org/reference/archive/mao/selected-works/volume-1/mswv1_17.htm>.]

> really the inverse. Knowledge presupposes the practical moment of surrender. The Maoist principle 'it is right to rebel'[40] becomes the following in Hegel: it is right to surrender ourselves to [the life of the object] and the connection Hegel→Mao shown above becomes much more contradictory.

If then in traversing the Hegelian advice (it is necessary to surrender ourselves to the life of the object) we can conceive of a unity between Marxism and Hegel, who both maintain that practice is a condition internal to theory itself, something changes in taking the question of practice into account in each case: for a Marxist, it is the revolt against the reactionaries that is the internal anchoring of theory, and for Hegel, it is conversely the internal practice of surrender that will be adequate to knowing. This is reformulated in saying, '...all that is needed is to ensure that the beginning remains immanent to its scientific development is to consider, or rather, ridding oneself of all other reflections and opinions whatever, simply to take up, *what is there before us*'.[41]

40. [The Cultural Revolution slogan '革命無罪, 造反有理' literally means 'there is no crime in revolution, there is reason to revolt/rebel'. It is often and condensed to the English phrase 'it is right to rebel' and the slightly more accurate French phrase, '*On a raison de se revolter*'. While the French emphasizes the reason of revolt, rather than the ambiguous notion of 'right' in the English, the legal sense of 'right' is in fact invoked in a negative sense in the first half of the slogan.]

41. [Hegel, *Science of Logic*, p. 69.]

(m) A synthesis on the materialist dialectic

In the following chapter (a chapter un-translated here and entitled 'The conception of Hegel relative to the process of development of the whole of the world'), the author, attempting to cut off the idealist deformations of the Hegelian dialectic, aims at taking up the idea according to which:

> The internal contradiction of the philosophy of Hegel resides between the progressive and revolutionary aspect of his philosophy and its conservative, even reactionary aspect; more concretely that which enters into contradiction with the Hegelian idealist system does not designate the whole of the idealist dialectic, which forms an all with the idealist system, but designates only a 'rational kernel' of his dialectic, insofar as his idealist dialectic divine the dialectic of things and the objective phenomena themselves.

In treating the decisive question of the relation between dialectic and idealism in the Hegelian enterprise, Zhang introduces three notions:

- concerning the 'idealist system'
- concerning the 'idealist dialectic'
- concerning the 'rational kernel'

The articulation of these three notions is thus the following: The contradiction proper to Hegel's work does not oppose idealism (as system) to the dialectic, but idealism to the rational kernel. The third term (the Hegelian dialectic) is the result of this contradiction.

This point is decisive in that it indicates that the idealist mark is internal to the dialectic itself. Thus what opens up is the path of a divided reading of Hegel. This reading does not oppose the dialectic to idealism for the evident reason that the contrary to the dialectic has never been idealism, but rather metaphysics. The true division of Hegel is necessarily the opposition, internal to its dialectic, of idealism and materialism, that is to say, the opposition of the effects of the system and the rational kernel. Otherwise put, the rational kernel of the Hegelian dialectic is necessarily materialism.

Thus, in Hegel's work there is a materialist (and dialectic) path that properly designates the rational kernel, the 'critical and revolutionary' dimension of his work. This path is counter-posed, in an internal way, with respect to the dialectic, by its idealist contrary. This contradiction is at work *everywhere*, at all times in the Hegelian dialectic.

In a certain way, it is really this principle of reading that Zhang seems to put at work here when he examines the idea of movement in Hegel. Hence, to briefly summarize and take up the contradiction that he denounces:

Idealist system/Dialectic

Idealism/Rational kernel

We might say that, by idealist system, the author understands, 'at the entry', 'a self realization of the Concept, of the Absolute...' and faced with this aspect of the Hegelian idealist system, the dialectic is found to be limited: once the absolute is realized, there is no longer contradiction or movement, says Zhang, while dividing the Hegelian dialectic in an idealist aspect (finishing with the absolute), that is in reality a part of the idealist system, and a rational aspect (as it were, basically, whenever there is movement).

This gives us:

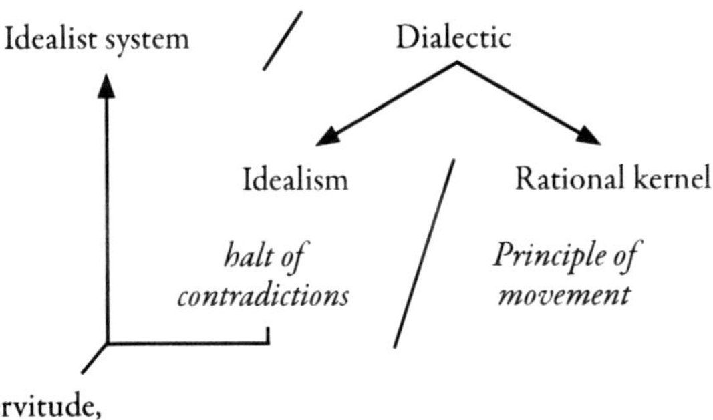

By this detour, there is no doubt that we demonstrate one of the contradictions of the Hegelian dialectic. However, we clearly see in proceeding in this way that we do not really obtain a division of the idea of movement in Hegel. The aspect of movement, full of itself, finds itself placed entirely on the side of the 'rational kernel'. For Hegel, the rational kernel and movement are then equated without knowing what type of movement is in question.

In this, we can explain the servitude of the dialectic in part, but all this is exterior to movement itself. In this step back into idealism, we do not perceive the internal causes to movement and, left aside, this latter will be seen as positivized.

In this, our attempt with Hegel consists precisely in advancing on [the question of] movement and hence on the dialectic, to see the consistence of the dialectic while traversing what Hegel said or practiced in the movement and the development of these figures. The style of transformation at work in Hegel is what we should question and divide; to seize the two in some way, the dialectical-ness of the Hegelian dialectic, to see what eventually returns to the one in this movement.

This is a project that can thus deduce a principle that even Zhang saw fit to highlight: whether the form of the dialectic given by Hegel finds itself in servitude to his idealist system. It leaves us wondering if the servitude itself is nonetheless something of worth in the Hegelian conception of movement and transformation... the very means by which Zhang carried out his examination.

Also, from the very fact that this idea of movement should be at work in Hegel, we cannot then immediately conclude by totally validating a passage of the type being→nothing ... without stepping back into none other than the idealist dialectic.

To divide this beginning of the greater logic, we will then ask ourselves:

1. In what does this idealist as movement consist, concretely?
2. But equally: at the very interior of this derivation, what had Hegel nonetheless divined/reflected of the dialectic of things and objective phenomena? In brief, what are their rational aspects?

An Interview with Alain Badiou

From the 'Red Years' to the Communist Hypothesis: Three Decades of Dividing into Two

Part I

Tzuchien Tho (TT): First, I would like to begin by noticing that this book is one where the context is very important. So I would just point to three contexts.

First context: the text was published at the end of seventies, with respect to the dates, we can recall that these are really the directly 'post '68' years, following intensifications in the political situation, the *years of lead*. I will not leave out reference to the 'new philosophers' [*nouveaux philosophes*] who took the questions of '68 in a different direction. In China, after the regularization of the relation between China and the United States ('72), there was the death of Mao in '76 and the demise of the 'gang of four'. In Southeast Asia of course, the war in Vietnam reached its zenith and the Khmer Rouge took power. The list of 'events' (in the general sense of the term) may seem too long but I draw this superficial sketch of the historical context in order to understand what the global situation was for you in this work. In the declaration made in the beginning of the text, you have given yourselves the task of putting the struggles in China and Albania in relation to the situation in France for better 'fighting revisionism in France'.[1] Your proposal there was a Marxist-Leninist-Maoist line. It was a work that aimed to give 'life and sense to Marxist-Leninism'.[2] How do you evaluate this project today? I ask this question in two senses:

1. Badiou in this volume, p. 3.
2. Badiou in this volume, p. 3.

in the political or philosophical sense of the relation that you saw between France (or Europe) and China (or Asia), and in the sense of a rapport at the interior of a communist project.

Alain Badiou (AB): The context was in effect that of the end of what I call the 'red years' [*années rouges*], roughly between 1966 and 1976. For the militants who refused to rally around the dominant 'democratic' order, the priority was to affirm continuity and the most important continuity was a political, practical one. However the 'new philosophers' were treating a problem of philosophical continuity. I found it interesting, with respect to the dialectic, to rely on a Chinese text dealing with Hegel. This proposed at the same time a distance of time (returning to Hegel) and a distance in space (Chinese commentary on a great Western classic). What is finally remarkable is that the beginning of the political reaction, from 1976 onwards, turned out to be a global phenomenon. The coup d'état in China that would bring Deng Xiaoping to power would play the same role in China as that of election of Mitterrand in France, the rule of Reagan in the United States, Thatcher in England, etc. The book is one of the last signals emitted from a sequence that was coming to a close.

TT: A second context:

Another context is obviously your own trajectory. I might ask this question in the framework of a 'philosophy as biography'.[3] We know that May '68 changed everything for you, your 'road to Damascus'. In the decade that followed, was it a period of politicization? How should we understand the relation between this text on the dialectic and this politics? I recall that it was in *The Concept of Model* you made a denunciation against 'theoreticism'.[4] The *Rational Kernel of the Hegelian Dialectic*[5] text came ten years afterwards, preceded by *Théorie de la contradiction* and *De l'idéologie*.[6] Even if the theme of formalism continued to be there, it seems to me that your orientation had changed in this path of your thought. For example, the question of continuity and discontinuity had been treated in the earlier texts under the mathematical question of the infinite or incompleteness and in the later text under the principle 'one

3. See Alain Badiou, 'Philosophy as Biography', in *The Symptom*, 9, Fall 2008.

4. See Alain Badiou, *The Concept of Model*, ed. and trans. Zachary Luke Fraser and Tzuchien Tho, Melbourne, re.press, 2007, p. 3.

5. *The Rational Kernel of the Hegelian Dialectic* henceforth abbreviated as Kernel.

6. See Alain Badiou, *Théorie de la contradiction*, Paris, Maspero, 1975. See also Alain Badiou, *De l'idéologie*, Paris Maspero, 1976.

divides into two'. Has there really been a change? Might you explain this complex knot of formalisms between politics and mathematics in the context of this chapter in your 'biography'?

AB: The question is in fact one of a relation between philosophy and politics. Philosophy can be defined as the thought of the forms of thought. Before May '68, the principal paradigm of these forms was logico-mathematics. In the 'red' sequence, the paradigm was displaced toward politics. We thus inevitably encounter the question of contradictions, struggle, and dialectics. My problem had always been to maintain the formal acquirements of the period of the sixties without abandoning the power of political thought. Hence I looked for a synthesis between modern formal logic and dialectics in the Marxist sense. The principle result of this effort is contained in *Theory of the Subject*. The book in question was thus a step toward the *Theory of the Subject*.

TT: Third context:

Yet another context is obviously the text itself. It still remains rather mysterious how this work was produced. How did you (with Messrs. Bellassen and Mossot) decide to collaborate on this project through the 'Yenan' collection? What were the conditions for choosing this text of Zhang Shiying and in particular this book and this chapter? How did you work? Could you also comment on how this collaboration worked toward this rather strange and singular book (a political essay in the form of a philosophical commentary and a philosophical commentary in the form of a political essay)? Is there something to say today about this 'performance' (and not only a statement) of the principle 'one divides into two' undertaken in this text?

AB: It was Joël Bellassen, sympathizer of the Maoist organization [UCFML] where I was a militant, and member of a group of Maoist sinologists whose name was *Vent d'est* published a journal under this title, that told us about this text and in particular the part of it that we decided to translate.[7] Louis Mossot was one of my earliest students, who was also a

7. Vent d'est (The Wind from the East) is probably better known as the collaborative film project between Jean-Luc Godard, Daniel Cohn-Bendit and Sergio Bazzini under the guise of the Dziga Vertov group. A number of Mao-oriented political activists had however operated under this name, producing articles, pamphlets and organizing trips into China in the period immediately following the Cultural Revolution. The pro-Mao faction in French sinology during this period was apparently so strong during this period that René Viénet, a contemporaneous young sinologist connected to the Situationists and a critic of Mao was so severely ostracized

sympathizer of the UCFML, and with whom I worked on a number of questions. We were all very interested in the question of the dialectic and in particular the new contributions of Mao in 'On contradiction' and 'On the correct handling of contradictions among the people'. We thus decided to do a book between the three of us with a number of introductions and detailed notes. It aimed to demonstrate that the principle 'one divides into two' is not a gross generalization of the dialectic but on the contrary a subtle and new vision that overcomes the vulgar Stalinist interpretation.

TT: We have often discussed negation in the past so it is probably not a surprise that I find it as one of the central themes in this work. In this text, you write something very interesting: 'Formal logic is in reality an artificial construct [*dispositif artificiel*] (mathematics) that organizes formulae (the writing of formulae). Like all mechanic assemblages, this tool is itself without force: it does not "work" over anything, and thus does not deliver any sort of truth'.[8] The text I cite here is part of an explication of the difference between formal negation and negation with respect to dialectics. First, how do we situate the difference between your thinking about this in the past and today? One cannot ignore the large framework constructed between *Being and Event* and *Logics of Worlds* for nuancing and clarifying this question. In a recent text published in *Cardozo Law Review*, you distinguished between three (or four) forms of negation. Hegelian negation is obviously not classical. In the text you proposed that, 'when the world is intuitionistic, a true change must be classical, and a false change paraconsistent'.[9] Thus, first how should we pose the question of Hegelian negation in this distribution? In *Kernel*, we see, by the references to the bouquet of flowers, the poor over-burdened donkey, the questions of the conversion between quantity and quality. It seems to me like there is a thematic or motivation shared between this text and *Logics of Worlds*.[10] The questions surround that of appearance and the forms of change. Was *Kernel* an attempt to think what, under the question of the Hegelian dialectic, will eventually come to be treated differently under the formalism of categories?

that he had the impetus to produce a number of anti-Maoist films such as 'Can Dialectics Break Bricks' and 'One more effort, Chinese, if you want to be revolutionaries'. Joël Bellassen is today a major sinologist in the Francophone world and especially in the domain of Chinese language acquisition. His various textbooks on the Chinese are international standards.

8. Badiou in this volume, p. 62.

9. Alain Badiou, 'The Three Negations', in *Cardozo Law Review*, vol. 29, no. 5, April 2008, p. 1883.

10. Alain Badiou, *Logics of Worlds*, trans. Alberto Toscano, London, Continuum, 2009.

Outside of these references to the quality and quantity discussion, I would here point to some surprising correspondences between the two texts:

a. The discussion of the dialectic between life and death in *Kernel*, p. 42-43 and *Logics of Worlds*, p. 269-270.
b. The distinction between change and modification in a place, a localization, a site in *Kernel*, p. 50-52 and *Logics of Worlds*, p. 394-396.

AB: We have already remarked that *Logics of Worlds* is closer to *Theory of the Subject* than *Being and Event*. The book in question was a stage toward *Theory of the Subject*, it is thus not surprising that you would find these connections between this book and logics of worlds. In effect, the Hegelian dialectic which supposes a non-classical theory of negation is, in my view, closer to the logic of appearance, or phenomena, rather than the logic of pure being. In fact, Hegelian logic is a sort of mix between intuitionist logic (which refuses the principle of excluded middle) and paraconsistent logic (that refuses the principle of non-contradiction).

TT: The configuration of negation in *Kernel* provokes many questions concerning the theory of conditions. In the text, you aimed at a negation that 'works'.[11] This 'working' negation is dialectical and not classical. Are the opposed readings of negation between these two periods of your work a change of mind or is there a deeper synthesis that I fail to see? In a certain sense, the active aspect of the theory of conditions resonate with this idea, that there are real dialectical movements in love, politics, science and art in which negation 'works' under truth. However, in this text which concerns dialectics, the difference between politics and philosophy is not clearly delimited and thus makes me ask if important distinction that you make today between philosophy and the four conditions might be reconstructed under the question of negation. Is it possible to understand the question of the conditions of philosophy through the 'work' of negation in these different domains? This distribution between the fields puts an emphasis on the 'active character' such that the 'names' like 'politics' and 'art' becomes indifferent with respect to the truth procedures.

AB: Intuitionist negation, such that it functions at the level of the transcendental of worlds is already an 'active' negation in the following sense:

11. Badiou in this volume, p. 62.

there are a large number of intermediaries between the proposition p and the proposition non-p. Negation is thus a limit case for the whole series of possibilities, which goes from identity to complete alterity passing through all the degrees of qualitative differences. What is purely classical enters in two levels: in pure ontology (being or non-being) and at the moment where a truth procedure is confronted with a point (where one has to chose this or that without any other alternative). Finally, at the level of the subject, we have paraconsistent negations. In effect, the subject in fidelity affirms the event and the reactive subject rejects it. And yet they coexist such that the principle of non-contradiction is not on the level of ideological struggle. Finally, philosophy is in relation to these conditions and should assume that all real processes combine three distinct forms of negation. This idea of a negative complexity is already present in Mao for whom the treatment of an antagonistic (thus classical) contradiction passes by a correct treatment of contradictions among the people (thus intuitionist and paraconsistent).

TT: The engagement with the question of materialism is a central aspect in *Kernel*. In the text, one of the central arguments was against a 'dogmatic' or 'idealist' materialism held by Althusser. Evidently, for Zhang, this problem of materialism was even more central. The principal aim of his text was the critique of Yang Hsien-Chen, who had critiqued the theoretical/practical model of Mao after the Great Leap Forward. The question concerned the identity between thought and being. In this context, you proposed a 'working' form of materialism, that of practice and method, that is to say, a dialectical form, a materialism that functions 'from particular to particular'. In what sense is this form of materialism at work in your thought today? It seems pertinent to ask how the return to mathematical questions (in the framework of identity between thought and being) in *Being and Event* that may be understood as 'idealist' may be clarified in reading your earlier texts. Also, how should one read the new 'materialist postulate' proposed in *Logics of Worlds* such that 'For any given world, every atom of that world is a real atom?'[12] Do we remain in the critique of Althusser as an idealist materialist even as we affirm a materialist dialectic?

AB: The most important project of Althusser was no doubt the definition of a progressive materialism which was nonetheless non-dialectic

12. Alain Badiou, *Logics of Worlds*, p. 574. See also *Logics of Worlds*, p. 220-221.

and separated from the idea of negation. The fact is that, as is in the case of Negri, he tried to attach Marx, not to Hegel but to Spinoza, a strictly affirmative philosophy wherein negation does not exist. In what concerns me, the principal line was always to maintain the motif of the subject, that which in effect makes the category of negation necessary. This is why my materialism leaves a place for a complex theory of negative operators: classical negation at the ontological level and intuitionist negation (thus a weaker one and why I name it 'inverse' rather than negation) at the level of being-there, or worlds. Having said this, I also maintain the affirmative dimension of materialism in its proper sense (dialectics begins above all with the truth procedures). The statement 'all atoms are real' does not make any allusion to negation. It rather says: at the atomic level (at the 'elementary' level of appearance) there is no distinction between a multiple-being and its appearance.

TT: In reading *Kernel* after *Being and Event* or *Logics of Worlds*, I had the impression that the question of contingency, a central concept of your more recent work, had not been taken up as such. The portion of the text where contingency is treated is in conjunction with the concept of deviation.[13] In what concerns the three terms, place, excess and destruction of place, in your recent seminars, the question of place or the '*hor-lieu*' of the ideal city of the *Republic* is treated under the concept of contingency and possibility or rather a possibility beyond simple 'probability'. Has the treatment of place, excess and its measure which have been developed at the time under the concept of 'destruction of place' been replaced today by an orientation toward contingency? Is there continuity between your earlier attempts and more recent thoughts of responding to the question of '*hors-lieu*' with respect to the concept of contingency? Here, I would also add the reference to Althusser who opposed dialectics and the aleatory in his final texts.

AB: I prefer 'chance' to contingency. We cannot call the relation between pure being-multiple and its being in a world 'contingent'. Certainly there is no strict relation of necessity or transitivity. Thought cannot deduce being there from being as such, contrary to what Hegel thought. But this non-deducibility does not construct an 'ontological' contingency. Thinking cannot pass from non-necessity to contingency, where (and this is Meillassoux's Achilles' heel) contingency becomes, in reality,

13. Badiou in this volume, p. 75-7.

necessary. In short, the only possible place for contingency in my *dispositif* is the event, but it is rather 'chance' in a non-probabilistic sense (there is no possible calculation concerning the event). Following this, there is a logic of consequences which is not contingent. The '*hor-lieu*' is the name that I have given to this non-necessity as non-contingency.

TT: And of course through the work of Quentin Meillassoux contingency has become a central question now. His way of approaching the question is very different from yours in terms of how the questions are posed. What do you think of this way of treating the concept of contingency? Is there finally a theoretical relation between the '*hor-lieu*' and the absolutization of contingency developed under the concept of the 'archi-fossil'?

AB: Contingency, for Meillassoux, is first of all with respect to the laws of nature. But for me, there is no 'nature' and thus no laws relating to it. There is an infinite multiplicity of worlds that the transcendental (and thus their respective laws) does not cover. This is the same reason why the infra-molecular universe is not made up of the same laws as the supra-molecular universe. The only interesting path here is the integration, in physics, of these differences in scope. We should admit that the scope of a phenomenon, thus the transcendental of a world where it appears, is an immanent given of its scientific rationalization. Fractal geometry permits the formalization of this point. After which we can let go of a uniform concept of a universe such as that of nature and of the laws of nature. This project is being brought to fruition by Laurent Nottale. In this context, the question of knowing if the 'laws of nature' are necessary or contingent loses its meaning.

Part II

TT: In the first question, I asked about the context. You responded in terms of the 'Red years', a turn towards politics and remarked that it was indeed in 1976 that, in China with Deng Xiaoping, in the United States with Reagan, in England with Thatcher, in France with Mitterrand, the 'Red Years' came to a definitive closure. Thus while this book may be fascinating for a researcher of the history of French philosophy, it is in some way, and I say this without any sense of provocation, somewhat forgotten. That is, there are people who know your work very well who may be surprised by the fact that you have written a book about Hegel. We might say that it is a little unknown. Thus, even as you speak of the problem of 'distance' between China and France in the 70s, so today there is a question of distance with the period itself. But there is at the same time also a real connection between China and France that is one of the legacies of French Maoism. What do you think of this temporal distance given the translation and publication of the text today? Has this sequence also terminated or is there something that we should rework?

AB: I think that first you touch on a problem that is absolutely important. This is the problem of knowing why French political thought undertaken in those years had been so linked with China, and why, today, this period of a connection with China has failed such that when I speak of it, it seems so bizarre....

TT: Right, there was even an article in *Libération* called 'Mao en Chaire' that focused on this strangeness.[14]

AB: Yes, absolutely 'Mao en Chaire'. If we approach the book in question as it stands in my project, my work, it is in effect forgotten, ignored, that is correct. But it is in reality closely linked with the *Theory of the Subject,* for example. And after all, there is not a single philosophical book of mine where there is not at least a chapter on Hegel. We could even collect all of these chapters into a big edition of collected writings on Hegel. So, intellectually, concerning the rapport with China, the Maoist vector was a major philosophical aspect. This relation is very different from the link with the Soviet Union. In the Soviet Union, Lenin or even Stalin were in reality political leaders in the strict sense. Whereas the figure of Mao was much more complex, in the figure of Mao there resides a philosophical reference and more precisely there resides a reference to contradiction, a theory of contradiction, and thus to the dialectic. I think that in the history of the Marxist aspirations of the 20th century, the Maoist attempt was the most dialectical. I am convinced of this. Stalin had rigidity... Mao was the most dialectical, one who searched for dialectical nuance. The fact that there was a book on the 'Chinese Hegel' at this point was thus not so surprising. Our central understanding of this Maoist link, in its political, ideological and other senses, was that Chinese Marxism,

14. This title signifies something like: 'Mao at the pulpit'. It also plays on the homonym chair, alluding to 'Mao in the flesh'. See Eric Aeschimann, 'Mao en chaire' in *Libération*, 1 October 2007, retrieved November 2009, <http://www.liberation.fr/grand-angle/010990542-mao-en-chaire>.

or Mao's thought, was an effort to transform the dialectic. And this political and ideological link, this transformation of dialectics, had its roots in Chinese culture. Yes, this is certain, just as the conception of classical Marxism had its connections with a background of German philosophy. At this level, the repression of this reference or this forgotten reference is also reflected in the problematic fact that the dialectic has long been abandoned in the main currents of the reactive philosophy in France over the last 30 years.... This repression [*refoulement*] cannot simply be attributed to the terrible totalitarian history of the contemporary China. I think the abandonment of the dialectical question ... or rather in the more general sense, the question of dialectics is something that I have continued to reaffirm and develop. After all, in the last large book, I opposed democratic materialism to dialectics. The question of dialectics has remained central for me and insofar as dialectics has remained a central question, so also this sort of attempt at the transformation of dialectics that took place in China during those years between the 30s and the 70s, remains close to me. I return to the question of 'distance' that you spoke of. We are not so distant from the particularities of the Chinese revolution today, not because we are confronting the same things but rather because of the dialectical kernel of thought that was at work within, including the rapport between dialectics and formalism, if I could put it in this way. This is [Albert] Lautman's fundamental question after all, I might add. But the fundamental question for Mao was: what is the rapport between the dialectic and the formalism of the Party. This was ultimately his problem. The party was a form, and above all a *form*. It was a form that almost crushes [*écraser*] the content, I would say. [...] The content of the thought of that period has not been overcome or resolved, the root of the failures of that period. And, on this point, this distance is in fact proximity. What failed remains as that which we should draw near, even if we do not know exactly where we are going—but it's just as well; it's not that important that we *do* know.

TT: Yes, your response is very interesting in that it responds to a sort of criticism that has always been made against French Maoism, a criticism that could be rephrased in Žižek's comment about the idea that we imagine that there is a genuine 'elsewhere', and we can take a distance from it and remain in our academic, western situation.[15] There something going

15. Žižek speaks of this in a number of different contexts but a published instance of this can be found in an interview with *JAC Online*. Slavoj Žižek with Gary A. Olsen and Lynn Worsham,

on somewhere else, in the figure of Chávez or the protests in Tehran, or Gaza or anywhere else. [...].

AB: Absolutely, that is what I think. We cannot simply understand those years as revolutionary exoticism, not at all. I think that Maoism brought about a real transformation of the questions. It is very interesting for its philosophical effects as well. Ultimately, Mao was someone who was very important in this sense. Brecht was already someone who had remarked on the 'Theory of Contradiction' for example. Here, outside the philosophical texts, we also need to look closely at the military texts as well. The military texts are fundamentally dialectical texts, if we look at the principle of strategic defensive.[16] It is an extremely dialectical question. From this we have two solutions, either the absolute abandon of this problem and it turns into a definitive distance, or we can consider these problems of dialectic and formalism still fundamental and still open. Here, we would take a distance and reduce it considerably, there is a contemporaneity to all this.

TT: And here the 'communist hypothesis' would not only be separated in time but also in space.

AB: Absolutely, there is a geography of the communist hypothesis. But also, if we take the Soviet Union in the 70s, there was no longer a communist hypothesis at all. Some might say that there was a communist direction, but it was finished, finished! For Mao, the question, 'where is the communist movement' remained absolutely a question. So for the communist hypothesis, it is not sufficient to just talk about communism but rather to truly animate the problem. It is without doubt that the communist hypothesis was animated in China. After this period of disparition, we are now reformulating the question, reconstituting the communist hypothesis, we might say, on a philosophical level, between dialectics and formalism. So there is a real temporal and spatial stake in the hypothesis and I absolutely maintain that China, in the 60s and 70s was a space of a singular and irreducible existence of the communist hypothesis which is no longer the case; but the contradictions carry on.

'Slavoj Žižek: Philosopher, Cultural Critic and Cyber-Communist', in *JAC Online*, vol. 21, no. 2, p. 270.

16. See Mao Zedong, 'On Protracted War' and 'Problems of Strategy in Guerilla War Against Japan' in *Selected Works of Mao Tse-tung*, vol. 2, 1967, Beijing, Foreign Languages Press, retrieved November 2009, <http://www.marxists.org/reference/archive/mao/selected-works/volume-2/index.htm>.

TT: In this case, does the *Tienanmen* incident have resonance with all of this? Recently, the memoirs of Li Peng have been collected and he remarked that seeing all the students and workers gathered in the square reminded him of the Red Guards singing the *Internationale*. Seeing the political speeches and such in the square made him fear that another sequence of this process would open up.

AB: Absolutely. With respect to the intervention of the army, I understand it [the *Tienanmen* incident] just in this way. I think it can be understood in two ways. The European understanding was that they were demanding democracy, etc. and they were put down by the Communist barbarians, like always. Another, more profound, comprehension requires us to examine the horizon of the Cultural Revolution. This is certain, we also need to represent the trauma that the Cultural Revolution left for the political figures and well ... everyone in China, but in particular the political figures involved, the masses and for the people in the party. So we might say that the repression was also sufficiently anti-dialectical, that is, against the return of the dialectical movement of things in a truly collective register. So there are two visions of the intervention of the army at *Tienanmen*, two opposed visions that does not need to presuppose that the movement had sufficiently arrived at a clear self-consciousness and comprised of a movement of greatly differing positions, just like the cultural revolution for example; a great disorder, taken on by Mao of course, who ... said that this was a disorder that will bring order.[17]

TT: It was a very mixed mass, like you said, and western-style liberalism was also part of this mass of anarchists, trade unions, communists, etc.

AB: Absolutely, there was a bit of every position. Just like in the Cultural Revolution, as we have seen, certain factions [of the Red Guards] were absolutely opposed, innumerable different tendencies working at the time. This story has not yet been completely written. [...] We have access to some of the documents now so the history of this period will begin shortly.

TT: I turn to another question. Well, a related question. When I asked you about the context of the writing this text, I asked a question

17. Badiou probably had in mind Mao's famous quip: '天下大乱 形势大好' (There is great disorder under heaven and the situation is excellent).

concerning the text itself. That is, the text is based around the proposition 'one divides into two'. Is it also not a *performance* of this idea? We have two long introductions 'Hegel in France', 'Hegel in China' and in the main text itself, there is division into two, the main text and the annotation. There is a sort of multiplicity within. So I want to ask if you intended to make a text in this way. I will also add another element. In this year's seminar, you have insisted on the essential impurity of philosophical discourse.[18] Here you have a great example of something like this. First you have a commentary on Hegel that comes from China, a sort of 'Maoist' commentary, and then you have a French annotation which is not always in accord with Zhang Shiying. There is a sort of dialectic which works through an impurity that is already in the text.

AB: Yes, it is true that the text, in its composition, illustrates the impurity of philosophical prose, and neither its form nor its materiality can be a homogeneous like a structured essay and here I cannot but just reply in your own words. That is to say, this was a work at a distance, we worked at a distance. There was a basis that was a Chinese text on the dialectic, and we know very well that it did not make much sense to simply republish it as such but rather to put the text into play in its proximity. It is at a distance since for the Chinese Hegel was something of a 'scholar', someone that came from the exterior, etc. We needed to approach the text and to close in on the distance so we presented 'Hegel in France' and 'Hegel in China'. Secondly we also annotated the text in such as way as to bring into play its distance and proximity in a divided way. The text is itself an almost material example of the dialectic between distance and proximity with a proper name that is, Hegel, but Hegel was nothing but a name.

TT: Yes, for this reason, the book is difficult book to 'read'.

AB: Yes, I'm not sure that we can really 'read' it. We might perhaps circulate within it rather than read it.

TT: For me, I first translated the commentary and then the annotation and when I started to put it back together, it gave me a whole different text. But this text is also the only one of yours that takes this form.

18. I am referring to Badiou's 2009-2010 seminars at the Ecole Normale Superieure, the third year of the series 'Pour aujourd'hui: Platon'. Notes and transcriptions, including this expression, can be found on Francois Nicolas' internet database, <www.entretemps.asso.fr/Badiou/seminaire.htm>.

AB: Yes, but I think it's the only text of mine that holds an effective contact with another text that is autonomous and at a distance so that imposed a form. But it was never our idea to make an introduction and then publish the text, we did not want an academic project, but rather a way to really show in what ways the dialectic was a central question in different spaces such that these different spaces, in showing the unity of the question, do not crush the distance but on the contrary ... how to show distance in a text? It is to show a gap between the introductions and the text, the texts and the notes, and finally we used all this to show what was at the same time a universality and a distance. It was ultimately a matter of localization, a localization in a text.

TT: Do you think today that it was successful, or is it an experimentation that was not sufficient in the end?

AB: Probably to say that we had a success would be to analyze the text further, take up the lessons and push them a bit further. In this case, it was a bit experimental. We started with the idea the Chinese were interested in Hegel, we were interested in what the Chinese were doing, and in the fact that they were interested in Hegel.... It was a back and forth, so we were first trying to show this. After this basic idea, we patched it up a bit, we fiddled with it. We made some notes to show our own conceptions, formal conceptions, so I think I would not say that it was a success but rather experimentation, an experimentation that we did not fully pursue and so it ultimately remains what it was.

TT: So was the idea behind this trilogy, together with *Théorie de la contradiction* and *De l'idéologie*, to make a larger book on Hegel? But ultimately, after the experimentation with this text, you moved on to *Theory of the Subject.* Was this latter project a synthesis?

AB: Yes. That is to say that I began, in the years before '68, a book project on Hegel, which would have been done with Hyppolite. This centred on the function of mathematics in Hegel starting from the large number of notes in the *Science of Logic.* I turned away from this toward politics but there was a trace of this, a trace ... a phantom of a book on Hegel. This was not really a book on Hegel since it is rather a book on the dialectic. It has a relation with Hegel through this Chinese book and so on, but it is really a phantom of a book on Hegel. This phantom persists today. There is a big chapter on Hegel in *Being and Event,* and of course also in *Theory of* *the Subject*. This book was written almost at the same time as *Theory of the Subject*, since *Theory of the Subject* was the course I gave at the same time as this book. Then in *Being and Event* and in *Logics of Worlds* there are also chapters on Hegel, so we cannot evade the fact that Hegel remains an important interlocutor in what concerns the dialectic.

But ultimately I reproach him on a number of points. I have never written a book on Hegel. Unlike Žižek who wants to write a large book on Hegel but who has not yet done so. He purports to bring it to us in the next year. But I think that Hegel did not succeed in really finding the dialectical point that is precisely the one between dialectics and formalism. Finally, his speculative formalism swallowed up the dialectic rather than showing it. Since this is my problematic, I am always nodding towards Hegel but at the same time showing the point in Hegel that de-dialecticizes the dialectic in the end. This is what I tried to do also in this book.

TT: This is the central point of the book, to divide Hegel into two: an idealist dialectic and a materialist dialectic.

AB: Yes, absolutely.

TT: Last time I asked you this question on materialism, which still remains unanswered. That is, your conception of materialism at the time was very linked to the dialectic and the way in which the dialectic is activated and then in your later works, like in *Logics of Worlds*, the meaning of materialism has shifted towards what you call the materialist postulate. So my question, again, is this. What is the relation between this materialism that is *in* dialectics, that is, a materialism that is only visible in dialectical movement itself and that always has two moments, an idealist and a materialist one, and a materialism in your later works which... if I may put it this way, is something more substantialized?

AB: I maintain that we enter into materialism through dialectics, and the inverse attempt will always fail because it cannot arrive at a concept of matter and that is the problem. Entering by way of materialism more or less paralyses dialectics and so entering by way of dialectics means finding a crucial point at the interior of the dialectic where we must decide to take a materialist orientation or not. I spoke in *Logics of Worlds* of a materialist postulate, that all atoms are real, but there we are aware of what we are doing, and we know what we are doing because we first entered by way of the dialectic. That is to say, by entering into the dialectic, we find the point where it must take the support to be real, that every atom is real. To assume that the support really exists outside of mind, consciousness, etc. and to do this in a precise way.... To arrive at the concept of the atom, we naturally need to enter through the dialectic, we need to enter through the movement of things through their categorical inscription and then through the transcendental and localization. Hence it is completely clear for me now in a way that was perhaps not totally clear to me before since I looked for a more general connection between materialism and dialectics. I did not have the operators to formalize these things. As for the precise statement, it means that we do not find materialism except in the protocols of the formalization of the dialectic. *Voila.* This also corresponds with my thesis that mathematics is ontology. There is being at play in the dialectics and it is presented in the moment where we take a decision on its formal character. This is where I am in agreement with Lacan, the real is an impasse of formalization. That is to say that formalization arrives at the point where we need to decide something. We are in an impasse when we are at a place where the formalization does not tell us what to decide, we must do it. There we are going to take a decision concerning the real that is a decision of thought as to its proper exterior. This is what I currently think. With respect to my thinking in the 70s, it was less articulate because, basically, the quarrel or the ideological struggle was rather internal to the definition of the dialectic: one divides into two or two fuses into one. What we can say about this epoch is that, if we adopt the synthetic vision of the dialectic, we will end up in an idealist vision and if we maintain that the fundamental protocol was division, we are open to other things, but the precision of the 'something else' that we were open to was not really given at that moment. So a path was opened up but it was merely the opening of a path

TT: Here, I agree. In my view the project of formalizing dialectics, whether local or global, was a project that was never fully accomplished. In other words, a level of formalization that can accommodate all the other forms of logic in a context needs to at least have a concept of dialectics that is at work within in. If I knew that you would say this today, I would have re-read Doz and Dubarle on formalization and dialectics before coming.[19] This project stops at a certain point, at *aufhebung*, an impasse.

19. See Dominique Dubarle and Andre Doz, *Logique et dialectique*, Paris, Larousse, 1971.

AB: Absolutely, in my view [...] we need to have a project that formalizes the dialectic. What I call the formalization of the dialectic is a project that is rather a development of the dialectic up to the point where we can see where the impasse is. And so we can see where we must decide, where things do not follow. Hence to arrive at this point, one cannot simply begin with the idea of formalization of the dialectic like what happens in Doz and Dubarle, it takes place too much from the exterior. It is an interesting formalization, I'm not saying anything against the project, but it is an attempt that is a too much *après coup*, a bit too much of a formalization from the exterior. If we are to do something at the interior, we might present something like a mathematics through its formal correlations or its formal constructions, just to the point where we are obliged to take a materialist decision.

TT: Here I move to a question that is a bit more of an aside, to the question of contingency and chance. In your answer you remarked that you would rather speak of chance rather than contingency. But just to ask for some clarifications, no doubt, the idea of modality thought through the path of chance allows one to distinguish between chance and contingency. Here I would simply ask to rectify an understanding of your thought. We have two sides. On one side, a non-evental side, we have nature or ordered sets that holds a distribution between necessity and contingency such that there are contingent and necessary things. Then on the other side, that of the event, on the evental side of things, we have something that enters through chance. Is this a correct presentation?

AB: Yes, we could put it that way. There is a side of necessity and contingency that does not involve the notion of event. They are internal to the theory of multiplicity as such. But on this point, I think the more precise structure is what was given in *Logics of Worlds*, where we have the different scales of modification, fact, weak singularity and strong singularity. In this gradation, we can lodge a rapport between contingency and necessity that does not superpose the relation between event properly speaking and other forms of change. After all, a weak singularity is largely contingent, and this contingency remains a term in the general regime. So I agree with you that in the different dispositives, there is a place between contingency and necessity that does not cover up the distinction between being and event and this why I rather say 'chance', reserving contingency for the intermediate forms of 'non-necessity'.

TT: If I might take up some themes from classical philosophy, there was on one side, contingency and necessity and, one the other, also miracles. So the debate in the 16th and 17th century was how to organize all this. If I might put it simply, there were those who thought that there was only contingency and necessity and no miracles, and those who thought that there were the two but also miracles but also those who thought of things simply as continuous miracles...

AB: So finally the question of the relation between contingency and necessity and the relation between nature and grace became such that the classical metaphysicians can be classified according to the solution that they gave to this problem. There was a Cartesian solution, a Spinozist, a Malebranchian, a Leibnizian and so on. Absolutely remarkable... and I think we are in the same situation. There at times where I speak of grace or the miracle and it does not bother me at all. The old Marxists accuse me of being a crypto-religionist or a traditional metaphysician. It does not bother me because I think that there are not simply two terms at play here but three. It is dialectical. There is not merely contingency and necessity. Yes, both exist, but there is also a supplement of something that radicalizes contingency such that it does not constitute the same register.

TT: So, we might say this in contrast to Deleuze where everything is brought into the same context.

AB: Yes, in some ways, for him it is the dialectic of chance and eternal return, so for him as I have said, it was a thought of the 'One'

TT: Now Meillassoux's problematic is rather that of getting rid of the principle of sufficient reason and such that each fact is a pure facticity.

AB: Right, when the law is as such undone, it is as if the universe is at its origin a pure facticity and that it could be at any moment otherwise than it is. But evidently Meillassoux's attempt is to show that it is necessary that it could be otherwise than it is. Some might say that Meillassoux's thesis is on contingency, no. Fundamentally, it is a thesis on the necessity of contingency, a thesis that is much more peculiar. That is to say that it is exactly the contrary of Leibniz, a turning around of Leibniz. Rather than showing that nothing is really contingent, Meillassoux is showing that everything is really contingent. And that is a method that is just as strongly rationalist as that of Leibniz; that is the surprising part. Meillassoux says that we can really show that contingency is necessary. This exactly what Leibniz thought: that nothing *is* without a sufficient reason.

TT: He called this a hypothetical necessity from the position that God had put into action the best of all possible worlds. Perhaps with Meillassoux, we might say that it is a hypothetical contingency which shows that everything is contingent.

AB: Absolutely, if everything is contingent then everything is free, and if everything is free...

TT: Then is there an event?

AB: No, absolutely not. There is no event for him. But we need to wait for the publication of a second part of all this, and in the end it means that in this freedom, we can suppose the existence of a good that is totally without power, since it is not inscribed in any necessity. It is a good that available for all contingency, that is to say that it is ultimately a god but a god, as he says in his thesis, a god that does not exist, a god that *inexists*. Perhaps it would be too much for him that something exists, to exist would be a demonstration of power, but here he hesitates. He remains in the more logical part of the proposal that is, the negative critique of correlationism and the positive proposal of facticity.

Bibliography

Aeschimann, Eric, 'Mao en chaire', *Libération*, 1 October 2007, retrieved November 2009, <http://www.liberation.fr/grand-angle/010990542-mao-en-chaire>.

Badiou, Alain, *Being and Event*, trans. Oliver Feltham, London, Continuum, 2005.

Badiou, Alain, *Manifesto for Philosophy*, trans. Norman Madarasz, Albany, State University of New York Press, 1999.

Badiou, Alain, *L'Antiphilosophie de Wittgenstein*, Caen, Nous, 2009.

Badiou, Alain, *Le noyau rationnel de la dialectique hégélienne*, Paris, Maspero, 1978.

Badiou, Alain, *Logics of Worlds*, trans. Alberto Toscano, London, Continuum, 2009.

Badiou, Alain, 'Philosophy as Biography', *The Symptom*, no. 9, Fall 2008.

Badiou, Alain, *The Concept of Model*, ed. and trans. Zachary Luke Fraser and Tzuchien Tho, Melbourne, re.press, 2007.

Badiou, Alain, *Théorie de la contradiction*, Paris, Maspero, 1975.

Badiou, Alain, *Theory of the Subject*, trans. Bruno Bosteels, London, Continuum, 2009.

Badiou, Alain, 'The Three Negations', *Cardozo Law Review*, vol. 29, no. 5, April 2008.

Badiou, Alain, *Wittgenstein's Antiphilosophy*, trans. Bruno Bosteels, London, Verso, 2011.

Badiou, Alain, et. al., *Concept and Form: The Cahiers pour l'analyse and Contemporary French Thought*, ed. Peter Hallward and Knox Peden, London, Verso, forthcoming 2011.

Bosteels, Bruno, 'Post-Maoism: Badiou and Politics', *Positions: East Asia Cultures Critique*, vol. 13, no. 3, 2005, pp. 575-634.

Dubarle, Dominique and Andre Doz, *Logique et dialectique*, Paris, Larousse, 1971

Engels, Friedrich, *Anti-Düring*, Progress Publishers, 1947.

Engels, Friedrich, *The Dialectic of Nature*, trans. Clemens Dutt, Progress Publishers, 1934, 6th printing 1974.

Engels, Friedrich, 'The Peasant War in Germany' in *The Works of Friedrich Engels*, trans. Moissaye J. Olgin, New York, International Publishers, 1926.

Glucksmann, André, *Les maîtres penseurs*, Paris, Grasset, 1977.

Glucksmann, André, *The Master Thinkers*, trans. Brian Pearce, New York, Harper and Row, 1980.

Hegel, Georg Wilhem Fredrich, *Elements of the Philosophy of Right*, ed. Allen W. Wood, trans. H.B. Nisbet, Cambridge, Cambridge University Press, 1991.

Hegel, Georg Wilhem Fredrich, *Lectures on the History of Philosophy*, trans. E.S. Haldane, Lincoln, University of Nebraska Press, 1995.

Hegel, Georg Wilhem Fredrich, *Logic*, trans. William Wallace, Oxford, Oxford University Press, 1975.

Hegel, Georg Wilhem Fredrich, *Science of Logic*, trans. A.V. Miller, Amherst, Humanity books, 1999.

Lacan, Jacques, 'Science and Truth', trans. Bruce Fink, *Newsletter of the Freudian Field*, vol. 3, 1988, pp. 4-29.

Lenin, Vladimir Ilyich, *Conspectus of Hegel's Science of Logic*, Progress Publishers, 1976.

Marx, Karl, and Friedrich Engels, *The Marx Engels Reader*, 2nd ed., ed. Robert C. Tucker (ed.), New York and London, W.W. Norton and Co., 1978.

Marx, Karl, *Capital*, Vol. 1, London, Penguin Classics, 1990.

Marx, Karl, *Grundrisse*, trans. Martin Nicolaus, London, Penguin Classics, 1973.

Mao, Tse-Tung, *Selected Works of Mao Tse-Tung*, vols. 1-5, Beijing, Foreign Languages Press, 1961-1977.

Mao, Zedong, *Selected Works of Mao Tse-Tung*, vol. 9, Secunderabad, Kranti Publications, undated.

Revolutionary Mass Criticism Writing Group, *Three Major Struggles on China's Philosophical Front*, Beijing, Foreign Languages Press, 1973.

Žižek, Slavoj, with Gary A. Olsen and Lynn Worsham, 'Slavoj Žižek: Philosopher, Cultural Critic and Cyber-Communist', in *JAC Online*, vol. 21, no. 2, Summer 2001.

About the Authors

Alain Badiou was born in Rabat, Morocco in 1937. He studied at the Ecole Normale Supérieure in the 1950s and, from 1969 until 1999, taught at the University of Paris VIII (Vincennes-Saint Denis) before returning to ENS where he is now emeritus professor in the philosophy department. Much of Badiou's life has been shaped by his dedication to the consequences of the May 1968 revolt in Paris. He has long been a political militant in a number of different organizations concerned with direct popular action in a wide range of issues, including immigration, labour, and housing. Alain Badiou is the author of several successful novels and plays, as well as more than a dozen philosophical works.

Tzuchien Tho has recently defended a Ph.D. dissertation on Leibniz and infinitesimals. He has published in many areas of philosophy and has participated in earlier translations and editions of Badiou's texts (*The Concept of Model* with ZL. Fraser also by re.press). He is currently associated researcher at Centre International d'Etude de la Philosophie Française Contemporaine at l'Ecole Normale Supérieure where he continues to work on historical and contemporary intersections between mathematics and philosophy.

CPSIA information can be obtained at www.ICGtesting.com
Printed in the USA
LVOW120435090512

280961LV00001B/157/P